BLACK COUNTRY
Memories 5

Front cover top: *Crowds in Queen's Square, Wolverhampton celebrating the coronation of King Edward VII on 9 August 1902.*
Front cover bottom: *Rowley Regis station in 1907.*
Back cover: *A view over Old Hill in 1961.*

BLACK COUNTRY
Memories 5

CARL CHINN

BREWIN BOOKS

First published by
Brewin Books Ltd, 56 Alcester Road,
Studley, Warwickshire B80 7LG in 2008
www.brewinbooks.com

ISBN: 978-1-85858-432-4

A Cataloguing in Publication Record
for this title is available from the British Library.

Typeset in Times
Printed in Great Britain by
The Alden Press

CONTENTS

ACKNOWLEDGEMENTS

It is a thrill to be writing a local history feature for the *Express and Star*. The paper is not only the biggest-selling evening newspaper in the country outside London, but also it is marked out by its commitment to its region and the people of that region. There can be few papers that are as local as the *Express and Star* and that commitment to localness affects positively every aspect of its reporting and coverage. The Black Country is fortunate to have a paper so dedicated to the well being of Black Country folk. I thank the editor of the *Express and Star*, Adrian Faber, and its management for giving me the opportunity to write so extensively about the Black Country. Adrian has been a constant source of support and encouragement to me and like me is a proud West Midlander. My appreciation is also due to Charlie Brechtman, Adrian's secretary, who carefully and thoughtfully collects all the memories and photos sent in to me and Dave Hotchkiss sub-editor, who puts together my pages in such a talented and sensitive way. I also thank the readers of the *Express and Star* who have honoured me by sharing with me their memories and letting me see their photos and precious memorabilia. All photographs are courtesy of the Express and Star unless stated otherwise.

FOREWORD

Carl Chinn is a modern day wonder. On the one hand, a serious historian with a vast knowledge of the heritage of the West Midlands. On the other hand, a human whirlwind whose energy and enthusiasm is breathtaking.

His understanding of the West Midlands is second to none. It has been a privilege and a pleasure to have him as part of the Express & Star team. His regular articles are undoubtedly one of the most popular parts of the paper. His legions of fans recognise the depth of knowledge he brings to his subject. He is a writer who has that rare talent of bringing the true human story to the vast breadth of history.

Oddly enough, Carl and myself have followed a similar path in the early part of our lives – growing up in the same part of Birmingham, going to the same secondary school and both attending Birmingham University. Now two Brummies have been reunited in the Black Country.

This is the fifth of our Black Country Memories books. The first was a sell-out. I shall never forget the queues of people in our front office waiting to tell Carl their stories and have their books signed. It was like a rugby scrum!

I am sure you will enjoy this new volume. It tells the stories of the people and places that have made the Black Country and the West Midlands the great powerhouse of Britain. The articles are sometimes funny and sometimes touching, but never dull.

Carl – thanks, mate.

Adrian Faber

Editor, Express & Star

Black Country Memories

I dedicate this to the people of the Black Country who have kept alive our dialect and whose hard work was vital in making England the greatest manufacturing nation in the world.

Chapter 1

THE BLACK COUNTRY

What's in a name? A lot, for a name is more than just a term to differentiate one person from another, one place from another. A person's family name binds him or her to all those before who carried that name, all those forebears whose lives are lost but whose genes and blood run through us and help make us what we are. Yes, of course each of us is a distinct personality and our upbringing and environment deeply affect us and help to make one person an individual – but we are not just isolated beings going through life separately. For good or ill we are fastened to those of our kin who came before, to those amongst whom we live, and to those yet unborn.

Just as much as we are part of a long line of family history so too are we linked strongly to the place to which we belong and which has helped define us. A sense of belonging and local patriotism has played a powerful part in English history. Loyalty to our county, our town, our district is shown in many vital ways, from our county regiments to our football, cricket and rugby teams, from our workplaces to our schools, from our places of worship to our municipalities, from the pub we drink in to the shops we spend in. We cannot escape who we are and where we come from. The Black Country is such a place that pulls its people to proclaim to it a strong allegiance, an allegiance that has been forged by a shared identity, shared history, shared experiences, and a shared language. Yet where is the Black Country, how did it come back, and what are the physical and historical forces that have played such a crucial role in making this place? Everyone will have their own ideas, but here are some of my thoughts on the making of both the Black Country and of Black Country Places. You may agree or disagree, in part or in whole – but that is the joy of digging and delving into our past and debating what is put forward. Everyone has an opinion, and rightly so for we all belong to history. It is ours.

The Black Country. We in the West Midlands know it is there but if you look for it on a map of England, Britain, Europe or the world then you will search for such a place in vain. If you try to find it listed in an A-Z of streets, towns or cities of the West Midlands then it will be to no avail. And if you key it in as a destination for the satellite navigation system in a car then it will be a futile exercise. Yet for all that the Black Country does not show up as a formal region recognised by map makers or by national government and for all that it is not a local authority in its own right, there are plenty of organisations that use the name proudly and prominently as a means of identification.

Black Country coal mines in the nineteenth century.

There is the Black Country Society, the Black Country Living Museum, Black Country Tourism, the Black Country Chamber, Black Country Observatory, the Black Country Bugle, the BBC Black Country website, and even a Black Country Urban Park. So the Black Country is there but where exactly? Therein lies a longstanding argument as to which places are in the Black Country and which are not.

Most definitions are broad and so try to avoid becoming embroiled in this dispute. They usually state blandly that historically the Black Country was an industrial region in the English Midlands lying just to the west or north west of Birmingham. There is not much there to disagree with but it provides no firm answer and indeed begs more questions. The Shropshire coal and iron fields were to the north west of Birmingham – does that mean they were in the Black Country? Of course they were not. The mines of Cannock Chase were to the north west of Birmingham – does that indicate that they were part of the Black Country? No, they were not, although there is a close relationship between the Chase and the Black Country. The hydraulic works, glass factories and carriage works of Smethwick were directly to the west of Birmingham – does that ensure that they came inside the Black Country? Well it is not certain – yes and no might be the confused answer, perhaps some parts were and some were not.

Many organisations also shun a firm description of the modern Black Country to try and evade fiery disputes that might arise as a consequence. They explain that today the Black Country tends to be taken as the metropolitan boroughs of Dudley, Sandwell and Walsall and the city of Wolverhampton. Yet although this wide-ranging definition is meant to get around controversy it fails simply because it is too broad and includes two places that historically would have been viewed as just outside the Black Country: Wolverhampton and Walsall. "Ah", might come the rejoinder, "but both now include towns that were in the Black Country." Yes they do, but does that mean that the Black Country is a dynamic, flexible concept? Some would agree, others would not. So where then is this place called the Black Country? Perhaps the place to start is with the origins of the name itself.

Back in 1803, Robert Southey was on a journey he did not relish. The man of letters who was later to find fame as Poet Laureate, was on the long and tiresome trip from London to the Lake District, where he was to stay with his brother-in-law, Samuel Taylor Coleridge, another celebrated poet. Stifled with fifteen other passengers in a long horse-pulled coach, he deplored the fact that he was enveloped in an oppressive atmosphere like that of a prison. Glum and becoming glummer, he arrived in Birmingham where he was made giddy and dizzy by the "hammering of presses, the clatter of engines, the whirling of wheels". His head aching from "a multiplicity of noises" and his eyes sore with "the light of infernal fires", he was keen to move on quickly and after just a day and night in Brum, he took a place on a fast mail coach to Manchester. It was a fair morning and Southey sat on the roof, joyous at freeing himself from the heavy cloud of smoke that hung over Birmingham and hopeful that he was travelling into a better atmosphere.

Heading west towards Wolverhampton, his high expectations were shattered on the anvil of industry. Everywhere, the "tower of some manufactory was to be seen in the distance, vomiting up flames and smoke, and blasting everything around with metallic vapours". The whole district was "as thickly peopled as that of London" and the houses were all blackened with the smoke of coal fires that burned both day and night". The poetic sensibilities of Southey were repelled by the marks of hard work, and he declaimed the face of the country as "more hideous than can be described, uncultivated, black and smoking".

This unflattering description by an unsympathetic outsider raised in fashionable Bath and educated at Oxford, drew together an area of South Staffordshire with a black landscape and buildings. He was not the first to do so. Just over a decade before, in 1792, John Byng, the Viscount Torrington, went on a tour of the North of England. On his way back home he came to Wednesbury. Like Willenhall, through which he had already passed, it was "an overgrown village, blacken'd with its trees and hedges, by the forge fires; nay even the sun himself is obscured by them!" Byng went to explain that "every field is scoop'd by collieries and canals; and the ironstone (happy distribution) lies under the coal. Iron foundries around are numberless, and the roads are made of the iron dross."

A generation later the Scottish historian and writer Thomas Carlyle reinforced the dark look of the Black Country and its people. In 1824, he spent several weeks in Birmingham with his friend, John Badams, a manufacturer of vitriol. One August day, he and three other companions left Brummagem for the neighbourhood of iron and coal works. It was "a half frightful scene!" From the description it would seem that he was on the southern side of the Black Country for he declared that "a space perhaps of 30 square miles to the north of us, was covered over with furnaces, rolling-mills, steam-engines and sooty men". A dense cloud of pestilential smoke hung over the district, "blackening even the grain that grows upon it; and at night the whole region burns like a volcano spitting fire from a thousand tubes of brick". In the coal mines locally, the colliers were "black as ravens", whilst the men who toiled in the blast furnaces were "besmeared with soot".

A decade later J. C. Young wrote of "the densely-populated black country". However although this statement is recorded for the year 1824 it comes in his memoirs published in 1871. Twelve years later in *Birmingham and its Vicinity*, William Hawkes Smith affirmed the black nature of the area, proclaiming that its inhabitants were "consistently employed in mining and in blackening manufactures" and that they were united by "a peculiarity of manner, habit and language". Still, though Hawkes Smith emphasised the blackness, he did not use the term the Black Country. By contrast, Carlyle did – although many years after his visit. In his *Reminiscences* penned in 1881, the Scot recalled how powerfully he had been affected by what he had seen to the west of Birmingham, and also brought to mind an earlier trip in July 1824. On that occasion, he and Badams galloped from Birmingham over to Hagley and the top of Clent Hill. Half way along, the friends came into a "wholly Metallic Country", of which Hales Owen was the heart. From the top of the hill were visible many smoke pillars "in a definite, straight or spiral shape – the Dudley Black Country under favourable omens".

Was then Carlyle the first to actually use the name the Black Country as opposed to describing the landscape and the workers as black? No, he was not. So who was then? We do not know, although the term black country is mentioned in the *Illustrated London News* of 1849. However, it would seem to have been the travel writer William White who made the descriptive term black country into the name Black Country. The author of books on walks in the Tyrol and holidays in Saxony, he also wrote *All Round the Wrekin*. Published in 1860, in Chapter II it includes a sub heading 'To the Black Country'. White enlightened his readers about this novel term.

The name is eminently descriptive, for blackness everywhere prevails; the ground is black, the atmosphere is black, and the underground is honey-combed by mining galleries stretching in utter blackness for many a league. The scene is marvellous, and to one who beholds it for the first time by night, terrific. Then the roaring-furnaces are seen for miles around pouring forth their fierce throbbing flames like volcanoes; then the hundreds of chimneys of iron-works display their blazing crests, or sheafs of fiery tongues; then the dull gleam of heaps of roasting ironstone makes you fancy that the old globe itself is here smouldering away; overhead dense clouds of smoke reflect a lurid light, rolling fitfully before the wind; while the hissing and rushing of steam, the clang and clatter of machinery, the roaring of blasts, and the shock of ponderous hammer-strokes, all intensified by the presence of night, complete an effect which amazes alike the eye and the ear. The effect is one that vividly excites the imagination, and is not easily forgotten.

The blackness of the Black Country was cast by its factories as much as were its iron goods. White also suggested that the Black Country itself was the smokiest end of Staffordshire, stretching for thirteen miles between Birmingham and Wolverhampton, and he made special mention of Bilston. Compelling and alert as was his description, because of the way he travelled White failed to mention Dudley, the town which would become accepted as the centre of the Black Country.

Two years after *All Round the Wrekin*, the satirical publication *Punch* published a disparaging 'poem' called 'The Queen in the Black Country'. This was to mark the visit of Queen Victoria to Wolverhampton to unveil the town's statue of her late husband, Prince Albert. The writer was not impressed with the loyalty of the citizens of Wolverhampton.

'Tis well his statue should stand so high, in this Black Country's core,
Looking across these cindery wastes, seamed, scathed, and ashy-hoar:
Where the eviscerated earth knows seasons' change no more,
Where the only seed is gold, the only harvest coal and ore.

Uninformed as he was, the jaundiced 'poet' strove to place Wolverhampton at the core of the Black Country. It was a position it neither sought nor gained.

By now the term the Black Country was taking hold. Punch's biting wit was followed soon after by a report in the *Daily Telegraph* of 1864 that "by night the

Dudley in the nineteenth century when it was regarded as the capital of the Black Country.

Black Country blazes up lurid and red with fires which … are never extinguished. Then in 1868 there appeared a more informed, thoughtful and positive depiction of the area and its people by Elihu Burrit in *Walks in the Black Country and its Green Hinterland*. The American Consul to Birmingham for the previous three years, he had been appointed by Abraham Lincoln himself shortly before the president was assassinated. Living in Harborne, Burritt was enjoined to report on the trade of the United States of America with his consular district and to add facts about its productive capacities, industrial character and natural resources. He soon realised that a few pages appended to each report would not be enough to draw out the

A Black Country factory in 1957.

A view of Dudley Castle in the distance as seen from Waddams Pool in 1963.

characteristics of the West Midlands and so he wrote *Walks in the Black Country*. It is a fascinating and insightful work which highlights vital information not only on manufacturing, trade and commerce but also on public buildings, prominent figures, historical events and natural history. It also includes one of the most compelling and vivid descriptions of "this remarkable district", the Black Country.

One night, Burritt and a companion secured entry to Dudley Castle. After warily climbing the deep-worn and winding steps that closely hugged the circular wall, they reached the parapet where "a grand panorama burst upon us". Proclaiming that the best poet of the nation should put his genius under the influence of that spectacle, Burritt went on to draw a scene "which cannot be paralleled on the globe". A military writer might have said "it was the sublimest battle-scene ever enacted on earth; that ten thousand Titans were essaying to breach heaven with a thousand mortars, each charged with a small, red-hot hill".

Fixing his eyes to the north from his vantage point, Burritt looked down across the settlements of the Tame Valley. Half circled as this space was by the Sedgley-Rowley ridge on which he stood, the low ground beneath him was also closed in at its northern edge by hills upon which stood towns like Darlaston and Wednesbury. The whole prospect made:

> an embattled amphitheatre of twenty miles span ridged to the purple clouds. Planted at artillery intervals on this encircling ridge, and at musket-shot spaces

in the dark valley between, a thousand batteries, mounted with huge ordnance, white at the mouth with the fury of the bombardment, were pouring their cross-fires of shot and shell into the cloud works of the lower heavens.

Wolverhampton, on the extreme left, stood by her black mortars which shot their red volleys into the night. Coseley and Bilston and Wednesbury replied bomb for bomb and set the clouds on fire above with their lighted matches. Oldbury, Albion, and Smethwick, on the right plied their heavy breachers at the iron-works on the other side; while West Bromwich and distant Walsall showed that their men were standing as bravely to their guns, and that their guns were charged to the muzzle with the grape and canister of the mine. The canals, twisting and crossing through the field of battle, showed by patches in the light like bleeding veins.

At the right centre of the line, the Brades Works of Oldbury discharged a thousand spades, hoes, trowels and pruning hooks each hour. Further towards Birmingham "there was a well-manned battery that poured forth a shower of bolts and nuts; and

Roaring furnaces in the Black Country in the 1950s.

Tall chimneys and smoke in the Black Country in 1963.

Chance's great fortress was all ablaze, with its hot fountains sending out acres of glass to be parcelled into pans of every size". Indeed, the whole arena of action was working for the world, producing the thousand small arms of peace – from cotton hoes for Brazil to Harpoons for the Behring Straits, "and, for all the countries between, every tool used in honest labour".

Burritt regarded Birmingham as the metropolis of the Black Country, but for all the pronounced linguistic, historical, and geographical bonds between the two places and their economic interdependency he was mistaken. Birmingham was not in the Black

West Bromwich, on the eastern edge of the historical Black Country.

Bilston Town Hall in 1952 – Bilston was always regarded as in the Black Country.

Country. Amongst the principal towns of the district, Burritt went on to number Dudley, Wolverhampton, Willenhall, Halesowen, Oldbury, West Bromwich, Wednesbury, Wednesfield, Bilston, Tipton, Sedgley, Walsall, Smethwick and Stourbridge. Some of these are also contentious. Smethwick may be best looked at as the fulcrum between the Black Country and Birmingham; Stourbridge is often perceived as just outside the area – despite the significance of its glass works; Wolverhampton was excluded by its own people and their Black Country neighbours; whilst Walsall could be in and out. Coal from the famed Ten-Yard Seam came close to the surface in many western areas and actually outcropped at Coal Pool, Reedswood, and Corporation Street (formerly called Coal Pit Lane); however by the nineteenth century Walsall was perceived by many as just outside the Black Country.

So if commentators wrote of the district as a distinct entity from the mid-nineteenth century and named it so because of its murky atmosphere and blackened appearance, where exactly was it? Writing in 1883, the celebrated engineer James Nasmyth recalled the occasion 53 years before when he had left Shifnal and traipsed southwards. Arriving at Dudley, he asserted confidently that "I was in the middle of the Black Country". Undoubtedly Dudley was central to both the concept and reality of the Black Country – and the emergence of both was inextricably bound up with the mining of coal.

The digging of coal from the South Staffordshire Coalfield scarred and blackened the ground and its burning blackened both the air and the faces of working folk. It would seem then that the area of the coalfield determined the extent of the Black Country, allowing for the fact that Dudley was a Worcestershire island and that Halesowen and Oldbury were detached parts of Shropshire. More especially, the historical Black Country should be delineated by the exposed part of that coalfield and not the concealed sections, where deeper mines were sunk from the end of the nineteenth century at Hamstead, Sandwell Park and Baggeridge and which were outside the historical Black Country.

In the north the exposed South Staffordshire Coalfield begins below the Bentley Fault, which separates it from the Cannock Chase Coalfield. That would put Bloxwich just outside the Black Country with Pelsall, Rushall, Shelfield, Walsall Wood, Aldridge and Brownhills clearly beyond the boundary. Today all are part of Walsall,

Mrs Minnie Page's cottage in Moxley is ringed by smoke from underground fires. Moxley was towards the northern limit of the Black Country.

Queens Square Wolverhampton in 1944. Historically Wolverhampton was regarded as just outside the Black Country.

which is described as a Black Country borough. Willenhall, Darlaston, and Moxley are also constituents of that authority but all were firmly inside the Black Country.

As for West Bromwich it was just within the district, as it straddles the exposed and concealed sections of the South Staffordshire coalfield – and it brought with it localities like Hill Top, Greets Green and Great Bridge. West Bromwich is one of the six towns now making up Sandwell. Four others were securely in the Black Country. They were Wednesbury, Tipton, Oldbury and Rowley and they drew in with them Old Hill, Cradley Heath, Tividale, Langley and Blackheath. The last town is Smethwick and it lay outside the Black Country, along with places like Bearwood and Warley. Just across the Western Boundary Fault of the coalfield, Wolverhampton never proclaimed itself as belonging to the Black Country and nor was it seen as such by its neighbours. As for the rest of the modern city, Tettenhall and Penn were most definitely away from the Black Country; Heath Town and Wednesfield were marginally outside; whilst Bilston and Bradley were obviously inside.

Dudley was the nineteenth-century capital of the Black Country, and the modern borough draws to it other places that were also strongly attached to the district. They include Coseley, Sedgley, Pensnett, the Gornals, Quarry Bank, The Lye, Netherton, Brierley Hill, Cradley, Wordsley, Amblecote and Kingswinford. Halesowen was thought by some to be slightly beyond the Black Country but was not because its Coombs Wood Pit was sunk within the exposed coalfield. Stourbridge was another borderline town but generally was thought to be not in the Black Country.

Yet whatever its boundaries, the Black Country was and is more than a place defined by minerals and work. Hawkes Smith understood that almost 170 years ago when he identified something singular about the people of the Black Country, fastened together as they were by "a

Walsall town centre – always just within the Black Country, although those parts of the town to the east were outside.

peculiarity of manner, habit and language". For a place is as nothing without its people. Carved out by their landscape as much as they carved it out in the digging of coal, limestone, fire clay and iron ore, and forged by their manufactures as much as they forged the metals crucial to their industries – so then are the folk of the Black Country tied by their sense of place, their understanding of their past, their awareness of their culture, and their pride in their language. Because of these strong characteristics, the Black Country is a place that becomes more than a geographical entity, infused as it is with a spirit that reaches out from those who have gone to those yet unborn. The survival of that spirit is entrusted to the living. Let not the bond be broken.

David Horovitz is the author of the monumental and definitive study on Staffordshire place names and his attention was caught by an article in the Express & Star supplement on Black Country Places, which:

"has encouraged me to carry out some further research into the expression the 'Black Country'. Perhaps the most significant volume, which must have done much to promote popular usage of the name, was 'Colton Green; A Tale of the Black Country, or the Region of Mines and Forges in Staffordshire', by W. Gresley, which was published in 1846. Although all but forgotten today, it appears to have had a wide circulation in the mid-nineteenth century. Whether that was the first printed reference to the expression is unclear, but it is likely to have been the first example where it is used in a book title. It's surprising that it should not be better known.

"In the Journal of the British Archaeological Society, 1846, the expression is found, whilst in The Youth's Magazine, or Evangelical Miscellany, published in or shortly after 1846, we find: 'Who shall count the number of the old, and middle-aged, and young, who are scattered through the pits and forges, and in the wretched cottages of this black country'.

"Then in the Ladies Cabinet of Fashion, Music and Romance there is a description of a railway journey, where 'We stop in the middle of a large station, full of life and bustle, and I get occasional glimpses of Birmingham: we tear through the Black Country … the furnaces, glowing in the darkness'. The date is uncertain, though is seems to be 1847 or soon after.

"The Tract Magazine; or Christian Miscellany, published in or shortly after 1848, includes the following passage: 'Early one morning, when living in Worcestershire, I heard the sound of many voices singing in unison, and on looking from my window, saw an open wagon full of hop-pickers, who, having finished their work, were on their way to the station to return, to their homes in "the black country", and were singing, as is their wont, while going along'.

"In the Civil Engineer & Architects Journal of 1851 or soon after is the following: 'It is from this viaduct that the traveller from the south will get a first glimpse of the coal and iron district so appropriately termed the Black Country'. Some idea of the area included in the term may be gleaned from The Christian Witness and Church Members Magazine published in or soon after 1856, which says: 'they preached in what was called "the black country", including Oldbury, Greatbridge, Walsall, Tipton, Gornal, Wolverhampton, and Bilston'."

David Horovitz's book is published by himself from Kiddemore Cottage, Brewood, Stafford, ST19 9BH and has the ISBN number 0-9550309-0-0. It can be bought for £45 (including postage and packing) from David.

Chapter 2

BLACK COUNTRY PLACE NAMES

Our place names call out to us to hark at what they are telling us, to notice those who gave them their names, and to understand their meanings. If we do but open our ears we can just catch hold of the men and some women who are kept alive in the names of many of our villages, towns and cities; and we can strain to hear how they described the features of the land in which they lived. Spoken and written countless times a day they may be, but yet how rarely is the significance of our place names appreciated. They are indeed our signposts to the past and like all good markers though they cannot take us on our journey they can show us where to go. If we truly wish to understand who we are and whence we come then it is on the path of place names that we must tread.

Some of them in the Black Country and in the adjoining districts reach deep into the beginnings of Anglo-Saxon England and even touch the times of the Celts before that. These British, the ancestors of the Welsh, have left their impression strongly on Penkridge in Staffordshire. Its modern name relates to Pennocrucio, a Roman station two miles south of the modern village. This was the Latin form of the British Pennocrucium which is made up of the Old Welsh words 'penn', meaning hill or headland, and 'crug', signifying a burial mound – traces of which can be found near to Rowley Hill Farm. Upper Penn and Lower Penn share the same derivation from the ancient word for headland, whilst the 'barr' in Barr Beacon and Great Barr also relates to high ground as it means summit or top in Old Welsh.

By contrast, Lichfield is a mixture of Old English and British, the forerunner of Old Welsh. The 'field' element is derived from the Anglo-Saxon word 'feld', meaning the open land or common pasture. This was close to 'Letocaiton', the grey or brown wood in the British language. From this word arose Letocetum, the Romano-British settlement that the Old English came to call Lycedd and which was pronounced as Liched. From the fourth century Letocetum had around it what the Old English called a 'weall' or wall – hence the modern place name of Wall nearby. Not far away is another intriguing place name, that of Walsall. The 'all' part comes from the Old English word 'halh' meaning the hollow or small valley of land; whilst the first part of the name recalls a man called Wealh. This meant foreigner in Old English and later became the word Welsh, signifying the Celtic folk who had ruled the area previously.

Lichfield Cathedral in 1844 – the city's name is a mixture of Old English and Old Welsh.

Then there is the most mysterious River Tame, perhaps indicating the dark river in Old Welsh, and itself arising from a pre-Celtic word. It was along the banks of this river and its tributaries like the River Rea of Birmingham that came the Angles who moved into the west midlands from the early 500s, fifteen hundred years ago. These people soon came together in tribal groups, one of which took its name from the River Tame. It was called the Tomsaetan, the folk of the Tame. Their territory included Lichfield and Tamworth and extended down Birmingham. To the west of them were the Pencesaete, the people who took their name from Penkridge. Their lands stretched south towards the Sedgley-Dudley-Rowley Ridge. Below them were the Husmerae, in and around what we know as Kidderminster. They have survived in naming of the district of Ismere.

These larger folk groups included extended family units who took their name from their founder or earliest remembered ancestor. Amongst them was Beorma whose 'ingas', people, joined him in setting up a 'ham', an estate or homestead. This became known as Birmingham. It may well be that Beorma and his followers

The mysterious and ancient River Tame at the bridge in West Bromwich.

Market Street Penkridge in 1982 – its name harks back to Roman times.

took control of an area larger than that of the old manor of Birmingham. Whatever the case, Beorma's folk would have arrived at a time when there was no great kingdom in the region and when the political situation was in a state of flux between the incoming Angles and the existing British. Another such kinship leader may have been Esne. He and his people, the Esningas, set up or else took over from the Welsh, a 'tun', a farmstead or manor. This was recorded in a document from 996 as Esingetun. It has changed but slightly to become Essington. Similarly Pattingham brings to mind the estate or homestead of the people of Patta.

From the early 600s the Esningas, Beormingas and larger tribal groups were brought under the sway of the Mierce, the boundary people. They probably took their name from the fact that they were the marcher people with the Welsh. Their heartland was around Lichfield and Tamworth in Staffordshire and under a ruler called Penda, who was in power till 655, a powerful kingdom called Mercia was forged. This fierce king is brought to mind today in Penda's ford, that is Upper Pendeford Farm and Lower Pendeford Farm close to Codsall. An even earlier Mercian king, Pybba, is kept alive in Pedmore, Stourbridge – this name meaning Pybba's moor or marsh. In old annals he is given as only the second ruler of Mercia, reigning for four years from 593.

By this time what would become Staffordshire, Worcestershire and Warwickshire were firmly under dominance of the Angles and thenceforth those Welsh who remained intermarried with the newcomers and slowly abandoned their language. Most of their place names were substituted by those in Old English and have forever disappeared. They were slowly joined by new settlements which had Old English names from the beginning. Then there were those places which may once have been called after a feature in the landscape but which were renamed after a man who was given the overlordship of a manor. Into this category fall Darlaston and Tipton.

The 'tun' element means a manor and experts have placed its common use to the period between 750 and 950. Thus Darlaston signifies the manor of Deorlaf. The second earliest recording of it was in 1262 when it was spelled it as Derlaveston, although by 1316 its modern form had emerged when it was given as Derlaston. As for Tipton, it was first noted in the Domesday Book of 1086 and was put down as Tibintone, meaning the estate of Tibba. Willenhall is mentioned much earlier and is one of the earliest Black Country place names cited in a document. In 732 it was given as Willenhalch and as such was the 'halh', small valley, of someone called Willa.

Sedgley and Dudley are two other places that remember men. Both signify a 'leah' or ley, a clearing – the one of someone called Secg and the other of a fellow named Dudda. Both places are amongst a noticeable number to the west of Birmingham which have this element 'leah'. They suggest that there was a growth of settlements through clearings in a woodland environment in the two hundred

Pinfold Street, Darlaston from King Street in the late 1960s. The town's name means the manor of Deaorlaf.

Cradley Heath High Street in the early 1900s. Cradley may mean the clearing of a man called Cradda.

years from about 750, in the same period that Deorlaf and Tibba came to be recalled in the manors of Darlaston and Tipton. As for Netherton, it was a manor named not after a man but because it was in a lower place.

There are also several names which may or may not be connected to a particular man. Amblecote means either the 'cot', cottage, of the 'aemel', caterpillar, or else the cottage of someone called Aemela; whilst Bescott indicates the cottage of Beorhtmund, as suggested by the spelling of Bermundescote in a record from 1273. Bloxwich possibly recalls the 'wic', farm, of Blocca; and it is likely that Cradley means the clearing of Cradda or Cradel, or perhaps the clearing where cradles were got for the making of hurdle fencing. Cradley Heath, therefore, is the heathland named after Cradley.

Women make rare appearances in place names, but one city in our region commemorates a noble lady. It is Wolverhampton. Lady Wulfrun

Amblecote and its gas holder in the early twentieth century. Has the name anything to do with a caterpillar?

was an Anglo-Saxon noblewoman, who was granted a 'hean-tun', a high estate. This was then called Wulfrun's high estate. Her statue stands close to the historic parish church of St Peter's, the porch of which is 529 feet above sea level, but who was this woman? Certainly, she was a person of some standing and was recognised as such by her contemporaries. She first comes to notice in 943, just four years after the death of Athelstan – the first king of England and the man who had led his Mercian and West Saxon fighters in crushing his Welsh, Danish and Scots enemies at the Battle of Brunaburh.

However, with the death of the mighty Athelstan, the Vikings regained their vigour and England was wracked by war once more. Led by the Norse king of Dublin, Olaf Guthfrithson, the Viking forces rampaged across the land and split apart the kingdom of England. Lady Wulfrun was one of the victims of the fierce conflict. In 943, Olaf stormed the old Mercian capital of Tamworth and as the Worcester Chronicle recorded, "there was great slaughter on both sides; the Danes had the

Crowds in Queen's Square, Wolverhampton celebrating the coronation of King Edward VII on 9 August 1902. The city is named after an Anglo-Saxon noblewoman called Lady Wulfrun.

victory and carried away great booty with them. On this raid Wulfrun was taken prisoner." Wulfrun was important enough to be mentioned by name and as a person of consequence it is likely that she was held for ransom by the Viking leaders.

Later freed from her captors, she is mentioned again over forty years later in 985, at a time when Danish raiders were again ravaging and pillaging. In that year, Aethelred, damned as The Unready, granted ten portions of land at Heantune and one at Treselcotum to Wulfrun in perpetuity. Remarkably the limits of her lands as given in this grant survived as the parish boundaries of Wolverhampton for over 800 years. They included the Goose Brook, a tributary of the Smestow Brook, which is recalled in Gorsebrook Road and where is found 'Wulfruna's Well', a memorial on the supposed site of an ancient spring. Other bounds were the Penn Brook and the Smestow Brook itself, given in its old Celtic name as the Tresel, which perhaps means strongly flowing and which is brought to mind today in Trysull

By the time of Wulfrun's charter the Anglo Saxons of the west midlands had been Christian for over 300 years, but importantly a few place names do commemorate pagan belief – and this is unusual in England. Wednesbury signifies the 'burh', fortification, of Woden and commemorates the leading pagan god of the early Anglo-Saxons. There is no definite evidence of a fort locally but there is a tradition that there had been an Iron Age fort on Church Hill and that a defensive site here had later been established by Lady Aethelflaed.

The daughter of King Alfred of Wessex, she was a warrior leader who ruled the West Mercians in the early 900s. In 910 she and her brother, Edward the Elder of Wessex, defeated the Vikings at the Battle of Wednesfield. The Anglo Saxon Chronicle gives the location as near to Tettenhall and there is a strong tradition that the fight took place on the Upper Green there. Be that as it may, Wednesfield also brings to mind the pagan god as it means the 'feld', open ground, of Woden. By contrast Tettenhall is the 'halh, small valley, of a man named Teota.

Remembered in Wednesday, Woden was regarded as the ancestor of the kings of the Mercians and was worshipped both in England and Germany, whilst he was called Odin by the Scandinavians. The creator as well as the god of war, the dead, and wisdom, he was also the leader of the Wild Hunt, sweeping his pack of baying hounds across the stormy night sky. In this guise he became associated with Father Christmas, for Woden also raced across the night sky in his chariot to bear gifts at the time of the winter solstice.

Both Wednesbury and Wednesfield are rarities, for they are amongst just 20 existing place names in England that refer to the old gods of the Anglo Saxons. There may have been more, but as Christianity came to hold sway over kings, nobles and then the common people, it is likely that the Church encouraged the changing of such names. Wednesfield and Wednesbury may have survived because the kings of the Mercians believed that they were descended from Woden, and the

Wednesfield – the open ground of Woden.

early Christians may have justified this survival on the grounds that he was not a god but an ancient warrior and the founder of his people.

Still it is not only the place names commemorating significant men or ancient gods that reach out to us; so too do those place names that tell us of the landscape of the West Midlands a thousand years and more ago. From the sixth century, when the Angles and Saxons took over the region from the Welsh, the new settlers looked with fresh and open eyes upon the physical features that they saw and named them accordingly. At Shelfield, for example, they spotted a 'scelf', a ledge or plateau on a hill. This is made plain by the earliest recording of the place as Schelfull in documents from the Later Middle Ages. In fact Shelfield does stand on a plateau with slopes on all sides.

At Caldmore the Anglian settlers found a cold marsh, whilst at Bradmore they set upon a broad 'mere', pool. At The Birchills they noticed many 'bircels, little birch trees, whilst they were struck by Merry Hill as somewhere 'myrge', pleasant. By contrast Pouke Hill was more forbidding and was associated with 'pucas', hobgoblins or sprites; whilst Wren's Nest was originally Wrosne and comes from

Caldmore Green in 1968 – Caldmore means the cold marsh.

'wrasen', a band or fetter. It may then mean a hill that was shaped irregularly like a pile of chains. Then at Alrewas the Germanic incomers sighted alder trees on a 'waesse', a plain that was liable to flooding – and so it still is from the waters of the River Trent.

Across what became the Black Country there are a marked number of place names ending in "al" or "all", from the Anglo Saxon word 'halh'. This meant nook and was related to 'holh', a hollow. Usually, it refers to a sunken place or recess, but sometimes it could be used to describe a nook of land between rivers, or for slightly raised land in a marsh. However, in the west midlands it is as a shallow valley that the term halh was most used. Today it is often difficult or indeed impossible to make out such a nook, because urbanisation and development have too often destroyed or obscured the original lay of the land. Exceptions are Shifnal in Shropshire, which can still be seen in a large, shallow basin that belonged to man named Scuffa, and Bednall in Staffordshire – the nook of Beda.

The valley associated with Walsall can also be made out – despite the overlaying of the landscape by generations of houses, factories and other buildings. Although its parish church, Saint Matthew's, lies upon a limestone hill in the centre of the modern town the ground falls away on all sides and there is a noticeable dip in the Bridge Street area, where the Walsall Brook flowed. Elsewhere in the Borough of Walsall lie other nooks or shallow valleys: Pelsall belonged to Peol; Rushall had

A view of Gornal – a name that remains puzzling.

rushes in it; and Blakenhall may have been associated with a man named Blaca or else was the settlement at the black nook.

Further south lies Halesowen, which for many years was simply Hales – the nooks. Certainly, coming down Mucklow Hill and with the Clent Hills before you, it is obvious that Halesowen does lie in a pronounced dip. Yet, as with Walsall, its parish church of Saint John rises from higher ground. The plural Hales suggests that there were nooks elsewhere locally, although much of the old manor of Hales was upland – as with the hamlets of Quinton (Ridgeacre) and Hill. Given as Hala in the Domesday Book of 1086, Hales was later owned by the Welsh prince Owen – hence Halesowen.

Gornal, both Upper and Lower, may have 'halh' in their names but their meaning is difficult to fathom out. Some place-name experts feel it denotes the 'cweorn-halh', the water mill. However as David Horovitz makes plain in his outstanding work on

Halesowen in 1958 – the town was once owned by a Welsh prince called Owen.

25

The *Place-Names of Staffordshire*, neither of the Gornals are in a shallow valley and Upper Gornal is on high ground. However, 'cweorn' could also mean a place where mill stones were got and in 1801 it was stated that excellent grind stones were dug at Cotwall End nearby. Cotwall itself signifies the 'cot', cottage by the 'waelle', spring.

A house in Ettingshall – the small valley of a man named Etta.

Ettingshall is definitely a 'halh, and is either the small valley of a man called Etta or else is the 'etting', grazing place. It belonged to Bilston, which was also mentioned in the grant by King Aethelred to Lady Wulfrun. It was noted again in a charter of 996 when it was written as Bilsetnatun. This spelling provides us with the full meaning of the name. The old belief was that it meant the 'tun', the estate, of Bill's folk. In fact, it indicates the settlement of the 'saete', folk, of the 'bile', meaning the sharp ridge or pointed hill. There is a possibility, however,

Rowley Regis station in 1907. Rowley signifies the rough clearing.

Bilston High Street in 1966 from the roof of a store. Bilston was the settlement of the folk of the sharp ridge.

that the Bil part may come instead from 'bill', meaning a sword or a physical feature that was sword-shaped.

Bradley was also part of Bilston. Given as Bradelei in 1086 it meant the 'braden leah' board clearing. It is one of that large number of names like Dudley that end with leah' which may assert the emergence of new settlements in a woodland setting from about the mid-eighth century to the mid-tenth century. Amongst the other clearings are The Lye; Rowley, which was 'ruh', rough; Horseley Heath, which had horses in it; Bentley, which had bent grass; and Langley. This means the 'lang' clearing and it would have emerged when the local folk said lang instead of long, as they do still in the lowlands of Scotland and parts of the north east of England. This pronunciation is sung every New Year's Eve when folk follow Rabbie Burns in his song, 'For Auld Lang Syne' (for old long ago). Indeed, the word lang continues to mean long in German and would have been brought to Britain in the fifth century by the conquering Angles and Saxon from their homeland on the borders of modern Germany and Denmark.

The name Warley is not so easily explained. Some experts feel that it is the clearing associated with a stream called Worf; whilst others assert that it is derived from either the Anglo Saxon word weofeslege or else weorfalege, both of which would indicate a clearing for cattle. Wordsley is another place that pulls us inexorably both into the nooks and crannies of English history and into the peculiarities of our place names. It is a clearing that could be derived from the Anglo-Saxon word wulfweard, meaning wolf guard. The first written record we have of Wordsley dates from the twelfth century when it was given as Wuluardeslea – a tongue twister for speakers of modern English. This spelling may also suggest that Wordsley might have a different origin, coming from the word wulfweardes, which would indicate the clearing of a man called Wulfweard.

Whatever the exact derivation of its name, for centuries Wordsley was part of the large parish of Kingswinford. Originally Swinford, the ford of the swine across the River Stour, it later gained the prefix King when it became a royal manor. Nearby Oldswinford belonged to Amblecote and was named Old to distinguish it from Kingswinford. A bridge later replaced the ford for crossing the Stour, hence the name Stourbridge.

Kingswinford – meaning the swine ford belonging to the king.

West Bromwich in the early twentieth century; it was given the name West to distinguish it from Castle Bromwich and Little Bromwich.

The woodland setting of much of the Black Country and thereabouts is emphasised by clearings associated with trees. Brierley Hill was the thorny clearing on the hill – thorny because of the briars and brambles thereabouts. At West Bromwich the Anglo-Saxons saw that broom trees were plentiful and placed a 'wic', a farm, amidst them. Interestingly, many older people still refer to it as Bromwich or Bramwich and it was first given as just Bromwic in 1086 – not being recorded as Westbromwich until 1322. It was prefixed with 'West' to distinguish it from Castle Bromwich and Little Bromwich.

Another 'wic', farm, was placed amidst the alders – hence Aldridge. This is the correct meaning as is indicated by the oldest spelling Alrewic and so Aldridge is not the ridge of alders as it may seem. As for Woodsetton, this was either the woodland 'seten', plantation, or else the animal fold in the woodland; Coseley was the clearing from which 'col', charcoal, was obtained; whilst Bearwood was perhaps the 'wudu', wood, where there was 'bare', woodland pasture for swine. Nearby Smethwick is the 'wic', farm or village, of the smiths. Mentioned as such in 1086, it emphasises the longevity of metal working locally.

Just to the north of the Black Country, woodland was a defining feature of Cannock Chase or Cannock Wood, as part of it was often called. Chase originates from the Old French word for chasing, hunting and hunting ground and Cannock Chase was just that

Sankey's Corner Burntwood in 1983 – was it where wood was burned or did the wood burn down?

– a great medieval hunting ground. As for Cannock it comes from either the Old Welsh word 'cnwc', meaning a hill or hillock, or from a similar Old English word 'cnocc' that means the same thing. Although Shoal Hill is nearby it is more likely that the hillock was the slight hill of gravel on which the settlement of Cannock was made. The spelling and pronunciation Cannock emerged from cnwc or cnocc because the Normans could not pronounce such words that were either lacking in or short of vowels.

Burntwood is also connected to trees. In 1296 it was recorded that the bishop of Coventry and Lichfield had 300 acres of common pasture in Brendewode. This was made up of the Middle English word 'brende', meaning burnt, and the Old English term 'wodu', a wood. It may be that wood was burned here for charcoal or that the wood itself was burned. In his book on Staffordshire Place Names in 1902, W. H. Duignan puts forward an interesting explanation for how Brendewode arose. He cited a Forest Jury of 1262 which found that "a certain heath was burnt by the vill of Hammerwich to the injury of the king's game". In the Middle Ages and afterwards, land was often cleared for cultivation by burning and it seems that this may have been what the people of Hammerwich did to nearby heathland and woodland, an action forever recalled in Burntwood. Three miles to the south west of the cathedral city of Lichfield, Hammerwich is yet another fascinating name. It is probable that it signifies the hammer work or trading place, from the Anglo-Saxon words 'hamor' and 'wic', and suggests some form of manufacturing locally

Burnt Tree Island has the same roots as Burntwood, whilst Brierley Hill means what it says – the wooded hill overgrown with briers. However not all place names are self-explanatory. Just as Aldridge can appear to mean something it is not so too can Great Bridge. There is bridge here across the Tame that connects Tipton and West Bromwich but the Great part of the name does not mean big. It comes from the Old English word 'greot' meaning a gravelly place. In the 1290s, mention was made in a document of Greet Mill. This stood further south of the modern Great Bridge, about where West Bromwich Street crosses the Tame. However, even earlier, in the late twelfth century, there is evidence of another mill at Grete, as it was spelled. Whatever the location of the mill, the name Grete became linked with the bridge, as documents from the sixteenth and seventeenth centuries make plain; whilst in this locality the Tame was also called the Grete Brook.

It seems that in this area, Greet could be pronounced Great for in a deed from 1556 mention was made of land 'between the King's highway leading from Greate Green to the town of Duddele'. Despite this, Greets Green continued to hold on to the old name of Greet, and was noted as such in the same century. Interestingly, a map of 1682 spells the place as Grits Green, as it is pronounced today.

Written as Owldhill in 1556, Old Hill is also a puzzle. Its meaning appears self-evident as old hill, but there lies the problem, for Old Hill is not on a hill. It has been

Smoking chimneys were still visible in 1972 in Greets Green – another place taking its name from gravel.

A view over Old Hill in 1961.

stated that originally it was called Old Dell and that because local people ran the
two words together its pronunciation sounded like 'Oldell'. This then became
became Old Hill. You do have to go up hill to get out of Old Hill, but local historian
Ron Moss reckons the name actually comes from Old Hall, an early name from
Haden Hall. However the mystery remains and although it is in a hollow, Old Hill
may be named after Reddal Hill or Haden Hill. Haden means the 'hean dun', high
hill and when we had forgotten that dun meant hill we added the word hill; whilst
Reddal Hill may come from the hill by the hollow ('halh') that was red.

Along rivers and streams came the Angles and Saxons who settled the west
midlands from the early 500s. They were struck by hills, hollows, valleys, moors and
plateaus, and they made clearings and created farms, villages and estates. The names
they gave to these places live powerfully on, drawing us into an awareness of the
importance of continuity in a world of rapid and perpetual change. We are who we are
because of those to whom we belong and because of to where we belong. If we are to
fully understand both, we need to clasp tight to us the significance of local history and
family history. Our places and our people. We are rootless without them.

Chapter 3

THE BLACK COUNTRY LANDSCAPE

As if standing guard, a line of hills stretches across the south of the Black Country, dominating the landscape. Rising just below Wolverhampton, they line up in a south-easterly fashion to begin with Sedgley Beacon and move on to the Wren's Nest, Dudley Castle Hill, Kates Hill, and the Rowley Hills. The high ground then marches onward, although more narrowly and less pronounced, out of the Black Country and across to Quinton and Frankley Beeches before going on to merge with the hills of Clent and Lickey. The Rowley Hills especially are a magnificent vantage point. Stand atop Turner's Hill and at 876 feet you are on the highest point in south Staffordshire with a spectacular terrain before you in either direction. Nearby are Oakham Hill and Corney Hill. All three hills are taken by some to be separate peaks of one Rowley Mountain, and by others as an "extensive range of hills terminated by several lofty peaks".

A modern view of the Rowley Hills, the dominating feature of the Black Country.

Looking from Church Street, Brierley Hill to the Clent Hills in the distance in the early 1960s.

There is an ancient legend that once, when the Anglo Saxons still worshipped the old gods, Thunor bestrode the Clent Hills. Red of hair and beard, and boasting great strength, he was the god of weather and is recalled in Thursday. Readily raised to anger, Thunor was a powerful deity. Wielding a mighty hammer he hurled thunderbolts from mountain peak to mountain peak when he was enraged. The story goes that he fought with his father, Woden, who is recalled in Wednesday, as well as in the Black Country place names of Wednesbury and Wednesfield.

One-eyed, all knowing and draped in his cloak and hood, Woden strode across the land when the weather was fine, but when it was stormy he careered across the dark sky at the head of a clamorous wild hunt. During the struggle between the two mighty gods, Thunor is said to have hurled a massive boulder at Woden, who had planted himself upon Turner's Hill in Rowley. The outcome of the terrible fight is lost in the fog of mythology, but Thunor's boulder came to be called Hailstone and so gave another name to Turner's Hill.

Of course, the Anglo Saxons used their tales to explain that which they did not understand, but what they did comprehend was the importance of the high ground in the southern marches of the Black Country. When they first arrived they must have been awe- struck by a wondrous phenomenon that belonged to these hills, for they lie on the watershed of England. On one side of the hills, rainfall drains south west via the Smestow and Stour system to the River Severn and thence the Bristol Channel and the Atlantic Ocean. On the other side, the water drains north east by way of the River Tame and its many small tributaries towards the River Trent and from there to the North Sea.

The Sedgley-Dudley-Rowley Ridge has an even greater importance, for the Wren's Nest in particular is renowned world-wide for its geology and fossils. Some 420 million years ago in the Silurian Age, the Dudley area lay in the middle of a tropical sea and therein lies its significance geologically. In September 1849, Sir Roderick Murchison, president of the Royal Geographical Society, gave at a lecture in Dark Cavern, beneath Castle Hill, Dudley. He proclaimed that "in no part of England are more geological features brought together in a small compass than in the environs of Dudley".

Today the Wren's Nest National Nature Reserve is rich in the remains of sea creatures that lived 400 million years ago, but it is best known for a fossil found there that is called the "The Dudley Bug". Properly this is Trilobite named Calymene Blumenbachii and it is at the centre of Dudley's former Coat of Arms. The reserve also

An entrance to the caves at the Wren's Nest.

Part of the Wren's Nest Nature Reserve.

has three distinct woodland layers (tree layer, shrub layer and ground layer) that provide the ideal habitats for birds and small mammals, and it is home to over 200 species of wild flowers. Indeed, it is one of the few places in the West Midlands where rare plants such as Small Scabious, Milkwart and Quaking Grass can be found.

Impacting greatly on the world of geology, the Sedgley-Dudley-Rowley Ridge has had as potent an effect on the making of the modern world – for it held beneath it the limestone and coal that were essential to the powering of the Industrial Revolution. In fact, the first record for coal mining in what was to become the Black Country relates to Sedgley in 1273. Another early working was that at the Foxyards, near to the Wren's Nest, Dudley, where the Ten Yard Seam could also be dug in open workings. Of course, coal came to be mined across the Black Country, covering as it did the South Staffordshire Coalfield, but the eye-catching hills on the south west were one of the richest sites for limestone nationally. Writing in 1883, the famed engineer James Nasmyth noted that after he had visited Dudley Castle decades before he had:

proceeded to inspect the limestone quarries in the neighbourhood. The limestone has long been worked out from underneath the castle; but not far from it is Wren's Nest Hill, a mountain of limestone. The wrens have left, but the quarries are there. The walk to the hill is along green lanes and over quiet fields. I entered one of the quarries opened out in the sloping precipice, and penetrated as far as the glimmer of sunlight enabled me to see my way. But the sound of the dripping of water from the root of the cave warned me that I was approaching some deep pool, into which a false step might plunge me. I therefore kept within the light of day. An occasional ray of the sun lit up the enormous rock pillars which the quarrymen had left to support the roof. It was a most impressive sight.

But if the heights of the Sedgley-Dudley-Rowley Ridge are the most dramatic feature of the Black Country landscape then they should not overshadow the rest of the district. Behind them is a plateau that fringes the Upper Stour Valley. Here are sited towns and villages like Brierley Hill, Cradley Heath, Cradley, Quarry Bank. All of them are marked out by steep rises and falls in the ground and the area is noticeable for banks such as Harts Hill, Primrose Hill, Homer Hill, Reddall Hill and Haden Hill. Netherton is another settlement hereabouts. Located in a drop in the land by contrast its parish church of St Andrew is reputed to be the highest in England and stands at 650 feet above sea level. To stand on its tower is an amazing experience because to the south west they reckon that on a good day can be seen the Bristol Channel.

If you move to the other side of the Ridge that divides the Black Country to face north eastwards and stand up on Kates Hill at night, you then look down upon the valley of the River Tame. The darkness is picked out by a multitude of lights from countless homes and factories below in an almost magical illumination. In the daylight, it is clear that this basin is broken up by low hills and ridges. Formed in most cases by glacial drift, they have not been eroded by streams. From early times, these

The view from Netherton's Saltwell Wood in 1982 before the Merry Hill Centre had been built.

hills attracted settlers and today we know them as Bilston, Darlaston, Wednesbury, and Hill Top. Just beyond them is the West Bromwich Plateau where is to be found the Hawthorns. The ground of West Bromwich Albion, it is 551 feet above sea level and is the highest of the 92 Premier League and Football League grounds in England.

Of all these hills in the Tame Valley, Church Hill, Wednesbury provides one of the most impressive viewing points for the Black Country and a counter balance to Dudley Castle Hill. It is a steep slope that is 537 feet above sea level and atop it stands Saint Bartholomew's, the parish church of Wednesbury, or the black church as some call it. A proud building it is now located half way between Junctions 8 and 9 of the M6. Tens of thousands of people speed by it each day on their journeys up and down the country, but how few of them ever wonder about the history of this church and of the town to which it belongs. If they had the chance they would do well to make their way to Church Hill and look down on the stunning views to the south west. There below are Tipton, Oldbury and other low-lying Black Country settlements and beyond them can be seen Dudley Castle. This is the Black Country – the watershed of England, plateaus and the valleys of the Tame and the Stour.

The Hawthorns, home of West Bromwich Albion Football Club, and the highest ground of a professional club in England.

Chapter 4

BLACK COUNTRY WORKING FOLK

Coal. Iron ore. Limestone. Fire clay. Casting sand. The five vital minerals below the Black Country that were essential to its rapid rise as one of the greatest manufacturing regions the world has ever seen. Coal it was that burned Britain into industrial supremacy in the nineteenth century. Burning in furnaces, factories, locomotives, steam ships and gas works it transformed the world, and in that remarkable change the thick coal of South Staffordshire was indispensable as a source of British power.

The Ten Yard Seam, as it was also called, was mined from at least the later thirteenth century, when it could be dug out from the surface or close to it. Just 21 miles long at its furthest extent and generally between six and seven miles in breadth, the South Staffordshire Coalfield may have been small but it punched well above it size. By the early years of the nineteenth century it was reckoned that between 500,000 and one million tons of local coal were burned annually in the works and furnaces of the Black Country. Within a few years, the Ten Yard Seam was second only to the vast Northern Coalfield in national importance and to show of its importance in 1851 a massive piece of coal from Tipton was exhibited at the

Brierley Hill from Amblecote in 1933 – a scene dominated by coal mines, clay pits and factories.

Great Exhibition in London. Weighing six tons, it was cut into a cylindrical shape six feet across by six feet high, whilst its surface was polished so smooth that it was like jet.

By 1872, 28,000 colliers were fetching out nine million tons of coal a year from Black Country mines, but long-term contraction loomed. Small mines became uncompetitive and others were flooded by water. Many closed. Deeper collieries were sunk on the edges of the coalfield at Hamstead, Sandwell Valley and Baggeridge, but they could not halt the swift fall of the Black Country from its pinnacle as a coal producing region. Coal continued to be mined locally until the

Miners in a pit on Cannock Chase in the late nineteenth century.

Sorting coal at a Cannock Chase Colliery in the 1950s.

later twentieth century but no longer was it king, and from the early 1900s the Cannock Chase Coalfield gained supremacy. By the 1920s more than 20,000 men in the Cannock mines brought up over four million tons of coal a year.

Wherever coal was to be found so too invariably was iron ore. These were were the potent twins that propelled Britain into industrial supremacy. Iron ore was smelted into pig iron in blast furnaces and that iron was then forged into an amazing array of products great and small goods ensured that Britain was unchallenged at the zenith of manufacturing nations, In the gaining and maintaining of that position the South Staffordshire iron industry was crucial. In 1839 Robson's Directory of Birmingham exclaimed that throughout the area:

> the roaring of the furnaces, the ear-piercing blast, the clanking of iron chains, and violent agitation of the machinery, the heat of the pavement, and all the innumerable noises incidental to such places, present to the view of the traveller a vivid picture of the poetical descriptions of the infernal regions. At night the country around is lit up by fires, proceeding from the various furnaces, forges, coalpits, coke beds, and lime kilns; while from a hill near this town, towards

Sedgley, nearly two hundred blast furnaces, for smelting iron from the ore, may be seen; a sight which probably cannot be obtained in any other part of the world, and in a dark night having an awful appearance.

Production of iron locally peaked at 752,000 tons in 1859. This was an amazing 22% of British production and it was blasted from 190 furnaces. Such a huge amount of iron needed to be extracted from an even greater amount of iron ore; and in 1866 it was reported that of the almost two million tons of iron ore was needed for the Black Country furnaces. Of this, over half was mined locally. However, the subsequent exhaustion of local supplies of both iron ore and coal led to a rapid decline in the number of furnaces to just 40 by 1880. Fortunately new jobs were created through the emergence of steel making in both Bilston and Brierley Hill – something which carried on strongly until the later twentieth century.

The mining of limestone, too, was in marked decline. Often overlooked in its importance, limestone was highly significant. In his *Natural History of Staffordshire* (1686) Robert Plot reported that around Rushall the stone lay in horizontal strata. It was broken up with iron wedges knocked in at the partitions with great sledges and then prised up with great levers. The lime was then burned in pits and after a week the layers of burnt lime could be shovelled out.

The limestone under the Wren's Nest and Castle Hill in Dudley was worked from at least the 1200s. By the 1860s these open cast mines were mostly worked

Workmen planting dynamite for explosions at the Wren's Nest caves.

out, after which the stone was got out via shafts sunk into the hill – as can be seen in the caverns today. It was then burned with coal in kilns, such as those still obvious at the Black Country Living Museum. This lime itself was used various ways: as a fertiliser; as lime cement, a mortar for building that arose from mixing lime, water and sand; and as quicklime, which was essential for the tanning of hides in Walsall. However most of the lime from Dudley was used as a flux in the smelting of iron to remove phosphorus, sulphur, and silica and other impurities. This led to the forming of the slag above the pure liquid iron.

Lime was also important in the refining of steel and in the making of glass. When it is heated with silica sand and sodium carbonate it forms a solution that does not crystallise when it is cooled. Instead, it hardens to an amorphous, clear, and nearly colourless solid, namely glass. The glass industry was one of the most important in the Black Country and it depended not only upon lime but also upon fire clay. All furnaces and hearths had to be lined with firebricks to retain their heat. Much of the clay in the Black Country was particularly suitable for this purpose, allowing blast furnaces and glass kilns to withstand the fierce temperatures so necessary in the making of glass and the smelting of iron. This clay was mined from local pits and was brought to the surface in slab form and 'weathered'.

This fire clay was fetched up mostly from Brierley Hill, Amblecote and Kingswinford. As for casting sand, that came from Bilston. Best known for its iron and later its steel, in 1851 William White exclaimed that the town was also noted for

A small pit in the middle of Bilston in the early 1900s.

"a peculiar species of sand, of a deep orange colour, so very fine that it is scarcely palpable. It is much used in the casting of metals, and is sent for that purpose to various parts of the kingdom."

A crystalline metal, cast iron is an iron alloy that contains carbon and is produced in a blast furnace – a substantial brick or stone structure, the interior of which looked like two cones or pyramids placed base to base. Great bellows forced air into the heart of the furnace where a roaring fire melted the raw material that had been fed into the top. The molten iron was then let out into open moulds of a pig bed, because its shape resembled that of pigs feeding from a sow. Once cooled, the pig iron could then be taken to furnaces where it was melted down and cast. This cast iron cannot be forged, rolled or welded whether it is hot or cold, but it was ideal for pouring when molten into moulds made from sand, the shape of which the iron takes when it cools.

Raw materials were indelibly bound to another feature of the Black Country – one that was made by man. Canals. The Birmingham Canal was finally finished in 1772. It went from Gas Street to Aldersley where it met the Staffordshire and Worcester Canal and in so doing connected Wolverhampton and Birmingham via the Black Country. Crucially it made the transportation of coal from places like

Loading coal onto narrow boats in Hednesford.

Wednesbury much cheaper. This invigorated Birmingham's manufacturing growth, which in turn created a higher demand for Black Country coal and stimulated its growth as an industrial region. Over the next few decades more canals, branches of canals, canal basins, and canal wharves were built to such an extent that it was said that you could not enter or leave either Oldbury or Tipton without going over a cut.

Fundamental as they were to the industrialisation of the Black Country, coal, iron, limestone, fire clay, casting sand and canals would have been as nothing without a sixth element – the people of the Black Country. It was they who hewed out the coal from ever deeper pits, who fetched out the limestone from cavernous quarries, who mined the iron ore from its depths, who dug the fire clay from its fields, who gathered the casting sand, and who cut out the canals. And it was they who made some of the finest manufactured goods known to man and woman across the globe through their hard collar, their deftness of touch, their alertness of mind, their ingenuity, their inventiveness and their innate craft. The Black Country folk made the Black Country.

Each town seems to be associated with some specialist trade that thrust its name on to the world stage through the prowess of its manufacturing folk. Netherton with its anchors. Cradley and Cradley Heath with their chains. Willenhall with its locks.

The anchor for the 'Titanic' was made at Noah Hingley's of Netherton.

Walsall leather workers splitting hides in 1962.

West Bromwich with its hollowware and flat irons. Stourbridge and Brierley Hill with their glass. Walsall with its lorinery and saddlery. Wednesbury with its tubes. Darlaston with its nuts and bolts. Tipton with its bridges and foundries. Smethwick with its optical glass, hydraulics and railway carriages. Bilston with its steel and lacquered and enamelled ware. Oldbury with its chemicals. Wolverhampton with its japanning and safes. Sedgley and Coseley with their nails. Wednesfield with its keys.

And just as these products reached across the world, so too did the names of the great concerns of the Black Country: Rubery Owen and Stewart and Lloyd's; Accles and Pollock's and Tangye's; Horseley Bridge and Chance's; the Bean and Kenrick's; Izon's and the Patent Shaft and Axeltree; John Thompson and Thomas Dudley Ltd; Eliza Tinsley and Albright and Wilson; Brockhouse and Lee Howl and Co.; Boulton Paul and Avery's; Chubb and Sons and Villiers; Cannon Iron Foundries and Goodyear; Samuel Taylor and Son and Doulton's. Just a few of the major manufacturers that made the name of the Black Country – but which could not have done so without the critical input of the men and women who grafted in these great factories and in the hundreds of little workshops, forges, mines and quarries across the district.

The lot of these working folk was a tough one. Britain was the most wealthy nation in the world because of the riches that overflowed from industrialisation, but that spectacular prosperity was not spread equally. The people who gained the most belonged to the elite handful of families who owned the land upon which the houses and factories were built and down through which the mines were sunk. In the Black Country, the Wards of Dudley and the Legges (Dartmouths) of West Bromwich took the biggest amount by far, whilst in Wolverhampton the Leveson-Gowers (Sutherlands) also profited handsomely as landowners.

Next came a few great manufacturers and well down in the sharing out of the spoils of industry were the small gaffers, shopkeepers and skilled men who were in regular work and who were well paid. Below them was gathered the vast majority, the working folk who grafted and scratted each day to pay the rent, stave off hunger, and get by independently. They gained little bar blood, sweat and heartache from a life of toil and moil.

In 1843, Thomas Tancred visited the Black Country for the Midland Mining Commission. He wrote that deep under the ground men, called holers or pikemen, sat on their haunches beneath the Ten Yard Seam and with their light picks hewed a

The sinking of Littleton number 2 shaft in 1902.

hole into the bottom measures of the coal. They stopped when they reached the natural parting between the lower level and that above it. To support the massive weight of coal above them they then built up cogs of stones.

Once enough coal had been undermined, the holers cut a gap between that section which was to fall and that which was intended to stand. In effect a pillar was formed to support the roof of the mine. Such pillars were made at both sides of the mass that was to fall and also at the end where it still joined to the solid coal. At the same time, small supports called spurns connected the undermined coal with the pillars. The cutting finished, the most skilful holer then hacked at the cogs and spurns with a long pick to break them away the so that tons of coal fell down in a 'throw'.

It is little wonder that mining was called the "hardest work under heaven", for the holers, or pikemen as they were also known, collared in a claustrophobic, oppressive and dangerous space. When it was finished a hole would be, perhaps, six foot long, three foot wide and just two foot three inches high. Young and fit though they might be, the holers might have to graft for eight or nine hours to finish their stint, contorting their bodies as they sat to pick away at the coal. Only the flickering light of candles tentatively challenged the utter darkness, whilst the only sound was the grunting as the holers shifted position or struck at the coal.

With the mass of coal removed, the holer stood upright to hack into the next level of the ten yard seam. Scaffolding was put up to reach the upper heights. This was "much more severe labour than holing". The upper body and arms of the holers were exerted so strenuously in the heat of the mine that one man declared that sweat streamed from them like rain. Deep beneath the earth and away from the strength of the sun, still it was as hot as a summer's day, so much so that many of the pikemen worked naked and were covered only by coal dust.

Often the pikemen had to jump back to avoid the throw of coal. One of them told Tancred that the operation was "worse than a field of battle full of soldiers, to be forced to go to draw the coals before it's settled and made secure. And, perhaps, the doggies (foremen) will say, 'Go in, we must have these coals drawn out.'" Accidents were as plentiful as the coal that was carved out from the pits. Deaths and broken limbs led to a loss of a vital wage for the man's family. There was no recompense for widows and disabled miners.

Mining remained a dangerous occupation into the twentieth century. On 21 April 1923, 57 miners working in the Dandy Mine in Pensnett were overwhelmed by disaster. About midday there was a terrific flood of water and the colliers ran as fast as they could to escape. Most did so but five men were missing. They were Ernie Haydon, a 40 year old married chap from Wordsley; William Simmons, another married man from Pensnett; Job Dando, also married from Bromley; and Tom Jordan of Coopers Bank and Enoch Cadman of Kingswinford, both of whom were single. They had been working towards uncharted, old tunnels.

Pensnett Church, where many people paid their respects at the burials of miners who had died in the Pensnett Disaster of 1923.

Rescue workers set to with pumping equipment, but made little impact upon the depth of the water. Worried people lined the nearby streets, hoping for good news. At last a rescue team made its way down the shaft. They located a live pit pony but found their way blocked by a tub wedged in the tunnel to the pit. Two days later, the rescuers found Enoch Cadman alive, sitting on a ventilation passage on the way to the thick coal. He had been in the dark for 48 hours and was clammed and worn out from trying to scramble out. When he saw the man who found him, Enoch exclaimed, 'Yo must be an angel, but yo've bin a long time a comin.' Unhappily, the four other men were found dead lower down. Thousands turned out to pay their respects when the men were buried in Wordsley Parish Church and Pensnett Parish Church.

They were harsh times indeed and if you did not work then you had no money, and if you could not earn then the only path ahead was that through the Archway of Tears and into the hated workhouse. Working people would do any job, no matter how low paid and dirty to hold back this indignity – jobs like chainmaking.

In 1896 the journalist and social campaigner Robert Sherard classed the chainmakers of Cradley, Old Hill and Cradley Heath as amongst "The White Slaves of England". When he visited the area he watched a woman spike maker labouring on her own in a shed fitted with a forge and anvil – on her own except for her child who sat in a tiny swing chair that dangled from a pole that ran across the workshop. That way the woman could grind away whilst she still minded her babby.

The previous week she and her husband had turned a ton of iron into spikes. For this tough work they had brought in the meagre sum of twenty shillings between the pair of them. Out of this they had paid 3s 8d (18 pence) for breeze, fuel, and the same amount for the rent of their home and workshop. On top of that they had been forced to spend one shilling to attend to damaged tools. That left them with just over eleven shillings (55 pence) to raise their family of five children. This was at a time when the poverty line was put at round about a pound a week for a moderate family. Worn out from slogging away, the mother was just able to ward off destitution and the break up of her family.

There was so much that was harrowing in the chainmaking district and yet the industry had never been so prosperous, at least if the amount of chain produced and workers employed were the indicators. Each week Black Country chaps and wenches made 1,000 tons of chain – chains of every kind that you could think of, from massive four inch mooring cables down to Number 16 on the wire gauge and including rigging chains, crane cables, mining cables, cart and plough traces, curbs,

Chainmakers at Noah Hingley's.

A female chainmaker in the Black Country.

halters, cow ties, dog chains and even handcuff links. In a moving and ironic observation, Sherard declared that "if chains for slaves are not made here also it is doubtless because there are no slaves in England; or it may be because hunger can bind tighter than any iron links. And chronic hunger is the experience of most of the women workers in Cradley Heath."

Like all chainmakers, the women workers heated iron rods – pulling the bellows for each link – then bent the red hot piece, cut it in on the hardy, twisted the link, inserted it into the previous link on the chain and welded or closed it with repeated blows of the hand hammer and the bigger Oliver hammer that was worked by a treadle. Female chainmakers mostly worked in small workshops or at the back of their own homes and made the lighter chain, although within the bigger factories where men made the heavy chain women and girls tended the bellows.

The female chainmakers did not suffer their vile conditions and mistreatment without fighting back. In his wonderful account of growing up in Cradley, the highly-respected Cliff Willetts stressed that "these women were as hard and as durable as the chains they made. They had to be, to endure the conditions in which they lived." Many of them were devout Methodists and sang the hymns sung by Sankey, the American evangelist who had visited England twice. From their number arose trade unionists avowed to improve the lot of their fellows.

In 1908 a woman's branch of the Cradley Heath Hammered Chainmakers joined the National Federation of Women Worker. Two years later many employers locked out their female workers who were fighting for better pay. The women trade unionists of Cradley Heath and district bravely took on the fight. A public appeal was launched to raise money and nearly £4,000 was collected quickly. Bolstered by this fund, the working female chainmakers were able to help their fellows who were locked out by the sweaters – and they were able to fight to the finish. After thirteen weeks they returned to work victorious, for every employer in the area had signed up to an agreement on pay. By 1914, the chainmakers were now earning 12s 4½d a week. It was still too little but it was almost double the sum before the Federation began its campaign of unionisation.

Anvil Yard, Cradley was a place where chainmaking families gathered. In 1888 the senses of an investigator for the Board of Trade were overwhelmed by the terrible conditions in this spot that was later cleared to become the Memorial Gardens. This small collection of overcrowded and insanitary buildings included fourteen houses and ten chain shops. The investigator noted that "in one case, a covered drain running past the end of a dwelling house, struck damp through the house wall from floor to ceiling; open drains everywhere carrying off household refuse and ruinous privies with overflowing ashpits, loaded the atmosphere with the most pungent odours. Here also are the little domestic workshops, built on to the houses, so that the occupants can step at once from kitchen to anvil."

Women of Anvil Yard, Cradley in the early years of the twentieth century.

Working folk lived in similar dire conditions in Caribee Island and the Tin Shop Yard in Wolverhampton, in Portobello in Willenhall, in Birmingham Street and Bond Street in Dudley, in Blue Lane in Walsall, and elsewhere. Despite these terrible conditions most working-class people strove to stay clean and respectable and forged strong neighbourhoods bound by ties of kinship and neighbourliness. Everyone lay on the same bed and most would share what they had with someone who had less – because it was the right thing to do.

Sharing the same lifestyle, the same hardships, and the same experiences the working people of the Black Country were tied ever more closely by their shared history and shared speech.

The Tin Shop Yard in Wolverhampton. Thanks to the later Mr G. Copper of the Wolverhampton Photographic Society.

The origins of their dialect reached back over thirteen hundred years to the coming of the Angles and Saxons to this land. "Ow bist?": heard still as a greeting in the Rowley Hills and also in the Forest of Dean in Gloucestershire it means "How are you?" The reply is simple, "I baint too bad". Both phrases are powerful expressions, harking back as they do to the origins of the English people and the beginnings of the English language. For the word bist is the German for "are", whilst baint is not bad grammar as some would claim wrongly, instead it comes from "be not" and as such is the negated form of the first person singular of the verb "to be". Such phrases have been spoken for almost fifteen hundred years in the Black Country and they call out to us that Black Country speech should not be demeaned and denigrated rather that it should be cherished and honoured and, most importantly, kept alive.

There are many words spoken locally that connect us forcefully with our forebears. When a babby is blartin we are speaking in the manner of the Anglo Saxons who settled hereabouts from the mid 500s onwards. For babby is from babban, meaning baby, whilst blartin derives from blaetan, signifying the bleating of sheep – and the noise made by a sheep can be compared to that of crying. Those Anglo-Saxon settlers would also have understood our use of wench. Coming from wencel, a child, it changed slightly to become a young maid. Today, when we speak of wenches we still mean young women, except in the case of Our Wench, who is a big sister who minded her siblings and acted as a little mother – and in the process gave up her own childhood and teenage years for the good of the family.

Boys in a yard off Birmingham Street, Dudley in the 1920s. Thanks to Dudley Archives & Local History.

Similarly, when we chuck something in the miskins, the dustbins, we are using a term that signified dung to the Anglo Saxons and which then began to mean dung heap. Of course, each village had a such a midden and, during the Industrial Revolution, when the country folk poured into Dudley and Tipton, Wednesbury and Bilston and elsewhere looking for work they brought this word with them, so that the miskins was the area in a yard where the rubbish was thrown. Later the name was adapted to the dustbins themselves when they were introduced.

If we demand of someone to "Get that down yer wassin!", their throat, we are clinging fast to the Old English word wasend, indicating gullet. If we talk of housen and not houses we are rightly adopting the old Anglo-Saxon plural of "an" and "en" rather than the more modern "es". And if we pronounce that we can't abear someone because we don't like them or can't endure them, then we are talking as did our ancestors who employed the word aboeran – and as did the great Elizabethan poet, Edmund Spenser. In his most famous work, "The Faerie Queene" (1590-6) he wrote in Book V, "So did the faerie knight himself abeare, And stouped oft his head from shame to shield."

Similarly if we refer to glowing embers or red-hot cinders from a fire as gledes then we bond ourselves with one of the greatest ever writers in the English language – William Chaucer. For in "The Reeve's Tale" he penned the lines, "Four gleedes have we, which I shall devyse." Regarded by many as the writer who beckoned Middle English into Modern English, Chaucer was not alone in using words with which we would be familiar in his plays. So too did Shakespeare. In the "Winter's Tale", Act IV, Scene IV, he writes "Clam your tongues and not a word more" – indicating clearly the need to starve the tongues of words. We know immediately what he means for in the Black Country clammed means hungry. In speaking such an expressive word we are recalling the German word klemmen, which means to pinch – and we can easily see the tie-in because of the phrase to be pinched with hunger.

Words such as this date back to the Mercian dialect, the language of the Anglo Saxons who settled the Midlands. After the Vikings conquered the east midlands, this speech still held sway in what is now the west midlands. Unfortunately, very few texts written in the Mercian dialect survive. Those that do indicate that an "a" into an "o" before a nasal consonant such as "n", "m" and "ng". Thus Mercians would have said mon for man, hond for hand and lond for land. It is remarkable that this feature has survived strongly into the twentieth-first century in the Black Country and

A woman in a yard off Birmingham Street in the 1920s. Thanks to Dudley Archives & Local History.

Birmingham. Our familiar word for mother is mom, whilst the urging of "Gie it some ommer!" means to give it some hammer, hit something with strength.

Following the Norman Conquest, the English became a subject people. Anglo Saxon became the speech of the conquered and dispossessed. Norman French was now the language of government, administration, literature and the Church – although Latin was used also in religious and administrative affairs. But the English tongue was not overwhelmed. Hardy and adaptable, by the later twelfth century it had evolved into Middle English – a form which is more recognisable to speakers of Modern English.

Flourishing among the common people, and now the first language of the nobility, Middle English burst fully upon the national scene in the fourteenth century with a wonderful array of literature. Each work was put down in the dialect of the speaker, for there was no such thing as Standard English. Emerging from West Mercian there arose a Staffordshire dialect which embraces Staffordshire itself, most of Cheshire, northern Shropshire, parts of southern Derbyshire, north-western Warwickshire and north-western Worcestershire.

Several major Middle English texts have been brought to us by people who spoke this dialect. Amongst them were Layamon's Brut, written about 1200. This poem tells the history of Britain and was written by a man who was the parish priest of Areley Kings in Worcestershire. Another important poem is "Sir Gawain and the Green Knight", written by someone who may have come from the borders of Cheshire and Staffordshire. He was also responsible for the poems "Pearl", "Cleanness (or Purity)" and "Patience" – all dating from the later 1300s.

"Sir Gawain" is an epic Arthurian poem and at its beginning a gigantic green stranger at King Arthur's court challenges any man to strike him with an axe "so long as I shall have leave to launch a return blow Barlay". Here barlay means free and unchecked and it is not hard to see how the word came to be used by kids in the Black Country and Birmingham in their play and when they wanted a break, as in a game of tig, or whatever, when a break is wanted and a child calls out "Barley" or "Arley barley!". The author also uses heo, which became her, instead of she and which is used often by us in phrases like "Who does er think er is?"

There are a number of other texts from our dialect region such as "Ancrene Wise", and "St Erkenwald". This last includes the use of the word brevit for reported. Coming from the Anglo Saxon word gebrefan it came to mean rummaging around, as in "I've been breviting and come across some good stuff". Perhaps the greatest Middle English work in our dialect is "The Vision of Piers Plowman", written in the later 1300s by a man who was probably brought up either in the Malvern Hills in Worcestershire or in the Clee Hills in Shropshire. In *The Vision* his affinity with our speech is proclaimed by the way in which words like banke are written as bonke, the "a" becoming an "o".

By the later 1400s, Middle English itself had developed into Early Modern English. Great changes continued to occur in the language before Modern English fully emerged in the 1700s. And changes are taking place still. However, despite the development of a Standard English in both the spoken and written word, the basic dialect map of England remains mostly the same as it had been in the Middle English period and so do the key differences between the dialects. Sadly though many Black Country words and sayings have disappeared or will disappear, just as the mines and big factories have gone and just as the old neighbourhoods have been swept away; and with the influence of television programmes and films, how much longer dialects can flourish is questionable. The Black Country and its people are in the throes of physical, social and economic change, but for all that if we allow our stories, our past and our words to disappear then we will have wiped from our lives the understanding of who we are and where we come from. We will become as nobodies with no past and no memory. Black Country history, Black Country landscape, Black Country speech and most of all Black Country people who have gone before call out to us not to forget our roots. Hold fast to them with pride.

Chapter 5

BLACK COUNTRY INDUSTRIALISTS AND MUNICIPAL PRIDE

Reuben Farley of West Bromwich. Joseph William Sankey of Bilston. Noah Hingley of Netherton and Dudley. The Chances of Smethwick. The Manders of Wolverhampton. The Owens of Darlaston. They are names that even now resonate with business prowess, economic power, social prestige and municipal endeavour. All of them were families that had become rich through industrialisation. They lived in grand houses, enjoyed prosperous life styles, and had the money to do what they wanted when they wanted. With an income way beyond even the most amazing dreams of the working people of the West Midlands, they could have easily withdrawn from the towns from which they had made their fortunes and abandoned the workers who had helped them to their wealth. They did not.

In contrast to so many multi-national firms today that have no loyalty to place and people and move their production to wherever they can pay the cheapest wages, these families did not cut and run with their money. They stayed in our region, engaging in local government, becoming involved in charitable organisations, and acting for the good of their fellow citizens who were not so fortunately circumstanced. Their commitment to their own localities was often inspired by the teachings of John Wesley and by the preachings of radical Non-Conformists such as Charles Berry. Minister of the Queen Street Congregationalist Church in Wolverhampton from 1883-87, he was eloquent, charismatic, thoughtful and inspiring. In particular, Berry was devoted to the idea of a Civic Gospel, whereby the rich would enter public life and work on behalf of the poor – so that all men and women, irrespective of their class, could be raised to higher living standards.

Reuben Farley – the embodiment of the municipal pride and identity of West Bromwich.

Dignitaries alongside a fountain presented by Alderman Reuben Farley at the Sons of Rest Pavilion, Farley Park.

The impact of this Civic Gospel was felt as strongly in the towns of the Black Country as much as it was in Wolverhampton, Birmingham, Manchester and Leeds. Many leading manufacturers and businessmen threw themselves into municipal activities. Reuben Farley was one of the most notable. An Anglican, he was as committed to social action as was any Methodist, Unitarian or Congregationalist. He bestrode the civic life of West Bromwich as if he were the Colossus bestriding the harbour of Rhodes.

Farley was typical of that small but crucial band of successful manufacturers that believed intensely in owing a duty to the locality from which their money was made. According to the *Free Press* of 1883, from when he was a young man Farley "unceasingly identified himself with all the principal movements having their object the progress and well-being of the town and its inhabitants". Born in Great Bridge, Farley's father died when he was five but by hard work and flair he became a success in business. He then moved devoted himself to the well being of the people of West Bromwich.

The Improvement Commission was the body that mostly ran the town before it became incorporated as a borough in 1882 – when Reuben Farley was chosen as the first mayor. Under his leadership of the Commission, West Bromwich had obtained

Farley Park, West Bromwich.

its own gas works, gained Dartmouth Park, built its Town Hall and other civic structures, and had adopted the Public Libraries Act on 30 November 1870. It was one of the first 50 places in the country to do so and was only the fifth in Staffordshire.

That was not the extent of Farley's remarkable commitment to the welfare of the people of West Bromwich. He bestowed the Oak House Museum to the municipality and was a county magistrate, the long-serving president of the West Bromwich Building Society, and a member of both the Board of Guardians and the first School Board locally. Unsurprisingly Farley was honoured as the first freeman of West Bromwich for he had "by his own ability, energy, and conscientious discharge of duty, together with his unvarying courtesy of demeanour, acquitted himself to the approbation of his fellow townsmen of all classes, without distinction of creed or party".

Reuben Farley made it plain that "it was a man's duty in his native town to do all that he could to improve the condition of the people, to make the lives of the people brighter and happier". He was not on his own. Joseph William Sankey, the pressed metal manufacturer, may have lived in Wolverhampton but his firm was in Bilston and it was to the betterment of that town that he dedicated himself. His father, Joseph, had started as a workman in a workshop that made tea trays that were blank, or unfinished. These were then sent elsewhere to be lacquered or enamelled and decorated.

Sankey eventually set up in business with two other workmates, but from 1861 he was in sole charge. He expanded into making hollowware such as frying pans, bake pans, shovels, and kettles, but it was under his son, Joseph William, that Sankey's became a giant of British manufacturing. In the 1890s, the company moved into electrical laminating. This became an outstanding success, although the making of trays, hollow ware and iron stampings remained important well into the twentieth century. Under Joseph Wiliam's energetic leadership the firm had also diversified into the pressed metal trade, which proved to be another notable achievement. The rise of Sankey's as a commercial concern was matched by the increased involvement of Joseph William in the life of Bilston. From the 1890s, he provided his workers with a mess room, recreation room, and workers' library and he later became chairman of the council, playing a leading part in public improvements.

Similarly, Sir Benjamin Hingley, of the great anchor and chains concern that made the anchors for the 'Titanic', was mayor of Dudley and a local Member of Parliament. His father, Noah Hingley, had much in common with Joseph Sankey, having been born a working man and having made himself by his own endeavours.

Hydraulic rivetting of field cores at Sankey's of Bilston – a firm whose owner threw himself into municipal life.

Noah began life as a working chainmaker, in Cradley, after which he rented a few chain shops. Somehow, he gained an order from a Liverpool merchant to make ships' cables. Never having made such a thing before, even so Hingley and his men turned out a satisfactory product. It seems that from this order, he moved into the making of anchors.

Noah Hingley worked hard for ten years to establish the trade. At first anchors were forged only up to twenty hundredweight, but with the introduction of improved machinery, forgings of up to 74 hundredweight were achieved. Soon Hingley's was making anchors not only for British ships but also for Indian and Japanese vessels. His success led him to move to new and spacious premises on the Birmingham Canal at Primrose Hill, Netherton in 1852. Within a few years, Hingley's had transformed the town to which he came to belong.

Noah Hingley – a successful businessman and civic dignitary. Thanks to Dudley Archives & Local History.

Noah Hingley himself was as noteworthy as were his anchors and he proved himself to be an astute and successful businessman. Determined to grasp hold of all the things that were essential for the production of his wares, he took on works for the making of the pig iron that was critical for the manufacture of wrought iron and he raised his own raw materials – coal, limestone and iron ore. By the time of his death, he owned the Netherton Ironworks, the Harts Hill Iron Works, the Old Hill Furnaces, and a number of collieries. Most importantly, he had ensured that Netherton would become the centre of the world's manufacture of anchors and cables. This was acknowledged by the British Government, for when the testing of cables and anchors for British shops was made compulsory the centres were set up both at Netherton and Tipton.

Hingley did not withdraw with his wealth into a private world. He enthusiastically entered civic life, becoming mayor of Dudley in 1869 when he was 74 – even though four years previously he had opposed Netherton's inclusion into its bigger neighbour. Throughout the district, he was regarded as someone marked out by his common sense. This "made him popular and respected" and he was ever keen to help the working class from whom he had sprung. For many years on New Year's Day Noah, Hingley "gathered together the poor and aged people and gave them a dinner, and 1s. each". A great benefactor and supporter of the High Town Ragged School in Cradley, his death in 1877 "drew the tears of sincere regret from thousands of the working classes of this neighbourhood; and the public funeral which was accorded to his remains, witnessed one of the largest gatherings of respectably dressed, sorrowful men, women and children that ever assembled on any occasion to pay their last mark of regard to real departed worthy".

Alexander Macomb Chance, the great Smethwick industrialist belonging to the world famous firm of glassmakers, also acted positively for the wellbeing of his locality. He was a remarkable man belonging to a remarkable family. Chance's, of course, was famed for making the glass for the wondrous Crystal Palace, in which was held the Great Exhibition of 1851, and for creating the finest optical glass for lighthouses across the world. However, the family name was also associated with Chance and Hunt, a chemical company in Oldbury.

Alexander Macomb Chance – a remarkable man who acted positively for the well being of local people.

Chance Brother workers repairing glass on Big Ben's clockface.

Alexander Macomb Chance had become its managing director in 1868. Like so many industrialists in the mid-Victorian era, he had an acute business head that was matched by an enquiring scientific mind, and in 1887 he was co-patentee with J. F. Chance for a process for recovering sulphur waste from the making of soda ash. Thereafter the company expanded and Alexander M. Chance became chairman. Yet he was not a hard-nosed, arrogant and bragging capitalist in the mould of Bounderby in Dickens's novel *Hard Times*, set in the mill towns of Lancashire. Rather he was a prime example of a successful businessman who believed that he had a duty to put something back into society – especially into the communities in which his family operated and from which they had gained their wealth.

Chance was responsible for a number of important initiatives aimed at improving the lives of his workpeople and their families, such as the building of schools, libraries, houses and a working men's club. Perturbed about what he saw as "the evil effects of drunkenness" and keen that he should set a good example himself, he became an abstainer from strong drink and formed the Langley Temperance Club. Active in the social work of the Church of England, Chance also built a convalescent home for his workers and set up a fund that quickly paid out compensation for industrial accidents on a no-fault basis.

In common with so many Christian employers who adhered to the Civic Gospel, Chance believed that municipalities needed to provide the facilities that allowed all citizens to recreate themselves spiritually, intellectually, emotionally and physically. This led him to become a staunch supporter of the provision of parks in which working-class people especially could walk, sit and contemplate God's beauty – indeed pass their time in recreation. To these ends, Chance played a key role in saving Lightwoods Park and Warley Woods from housing development. His cousin, Sir James Timmins Chance, was also active in many philanthropic activities. In 1895 and at a cost of £30,000, he gave Smethwick the West Smethwick Park; and in 1900 with another £50,000 he endowed the Chance School of Engineering in the University of Birmingham.

To the west in Wolverhampton, Sir Alfred Hickman was another noteworthy industrialist who 'put something back in'. An iron and steel manufacturer, he had been born in 1830 in Tipton and was the younger son of George Rushbury Hickman, an ironmaster and colliery. Educated at King Edward VI School, Birmingham, he went to work at sixteen in his father's business, which included the Groveland Ironworks and Moat Colliery in Tipton. He and his brother later took over the company, but in 1867 Alfred struck out on his own and bought the Spring Vale blast furnaces in Bilston. He transformed them and made the firm a leading producer of pig iron in the Black Country.

A moderniser who was keen to adopt new processes, Hickman quickly recognised the potential of the new basic Bessemer steelmaking process when it was licensed in

1879. With other Black Country ironmasters he organised a trial to see whether local pig iron was suitable for conversion into steel. Crucially, the new process removed the phosphorus from the slag. Impressed, Hickman bought three Bessemer converters and formed the Staffordshire Steel and Ingot Company, with a steel works next to his blast furnaces at Bilston. By 1900, Alfred Hickman Ltd was producing 3000 tons of iron and 1500 tons of steel annually, and gave work to more than 2000 workmen. He continued to install the latest machinery such as gas engines and his rolling mills were reckoned amongst the best in the world.

Powered forward by Hickman's innovative thinking and his open mind in adopting new techniques, his business expanded greatly. He also saw an opportunity to make money by selling the by-products of steelmaking, selling slag for use as railway ballast and ground slag as fertiliser. Through the selling of slag supplied to the Tar Macadam Syndicate Ltd (later Tarmac Ltd), he persuaded the company to build a plant at Bilston

Sir Alfred Hickman.

Sir Alfred Hickman's Iron Works at Spring Vale Bilston in the early 1900s.

Sir Alfred Hickman became president of Wolverhampton Wanderers Football Club.

and provided both the land and capital to do so. After his death, his son carried on the company but in 1920 it was taken over by Stewarts and Lloyds. Five years later the Hickman name was dropped.

Like Hingley and Sankey, Hickman created many jobs and provided an income for thousands of families. More than that, at a time when the iron and coal industries of the Black Country were in rapid decline he was a vital figure in the development of steel production locally. It was largely because of him the decline of heavy industry was staved off in the district until the 1980s. Feted as the 'Iron King of South Staffordshire', Hickman was Conservative MP for Wolverhampton West twice up to 1906. As MP, he championed Black Country industrialists and campaigned for lower freight charges. However, he was also concerned with the welfare of industrial workers and introduced a bill to provide loans to help workers buy their houses. Unfortunately it was not passed. Although Hickman lived as a country gentleman, he was committed to Wolverhampton. In 1893, he gave the town 25 acres for a park that was named after him and he became president of Wolverhampton Wanderers Football Club.

Hickman's commitment to his locality was surpassed only by the Manders of Wolverhampton. Brought to mind today in the Mander Centre in the heart of the city, the family had a dynamic effect upon Wolverhampton. They may not have played as big a role on the national stage as the Chamberlains of Birmingham, but there can be no doubt that they exercised as much authority and influence in their home town. Indeed, it could be argued that their effect was longer lasting and deeper than that of the Chamberlains, extending as it did over several generations and not just two.

Settled in Wolverhampton from 1742, the Manders began their rise with two brothers, Benjamin and John. Benjamin became a maker of tinned plate ware such as jugs, cups, bowls and coffee pots. Made of iron they were coated with a thin layer of tin to prevent rusting. He was also a japanner, covering wares with japan, or lacquer and decorating them in the manner of the Japanese. As for John, he was a manufacturing chemist and druggist who diversified into making varnish, japans and colours for the japanning trade in general.

A man of energy and intellect, he typified those early nineteenth-century industrialists who cast their eyes and minds wide over a range of activities. He became a manufacturing chemist, providing 'choice chemicals' for the London market; whilst his company was one of the first to trade with the USA, to manufacture gas, to light its factory, and to make calomel and the various mercury compounds employed in medicine, the arts and the chemicals industry.

An avowed reformer and Non-Conformist, John was also a town commissioner and worked for the good of the people of Wolverhampton in general. He died in 1827, leaving the great amount of £16,000. It was asserted that "he had been for

Charles Arthur Mander as mayor of Wolverhampton in 1936 – he was mayor twice and was awarded the freedom of the borough for his services to the town.

Sir Geoffrey Mander unveiling a plaque in 1960.

about fifty years a prominent friend of religion and education, for which he was not only unsparingly munificent, but indefatigably active. Many a widow and her family have owed the comforts, and many young tradesmen their successes, to his intelligence and generosity. The institutions which he founded will be his best monument, and the tale of the grateful his best panegyric."

The various businesses Mander came together as Mander Brothers in 1845 and through diligence, determination and dedication the family made the company a household word and the main producer of paints and varnishes in the British Empire. Importantly, however, John and Benjamin Mander had set for their descendants a high standard of integrity, ingenuity, determination, dedication, civility and civic duty. It was a standard that each generation proudly upheld.

Theodore Mander epitomised their commitment to Wolverhampton. He entered the business in 1876, but infused with a strong Christian faith and the principles of his family he also became deeply involved in education. Chairman of the school board, Theodore also became governor of both the local grammar school, Tettenhall College, and Birmingham University. A deacon and lay preacher in the Congregationalist church, he was elected to Wolverhampton Council in 1881, later becoming an alderman and a mayor. Theodore has also left a lasting legacy in Wightwick Manor. Built for him between 1889-93, it was designed by Edward Ould and is a superb example of an Arts and Crafts house replete with William

Morris furnishings. His son, Sir Geoffrey Mander, added to splendours of the house with pre-Raphaelite and late Romantic paintings and literary manuscripts. This wonderful building was given by the Mander family to the National Trust in 1937 and was one of its first country houses.

Sir Geoffrey himself was also imbued with a deep-seated sense of social responsibility. A Liberal member of the Wolverhampton Borough Council for nine years from 1911, on one occasion he shocked fellow councillors when he proposed a minimum wage of 23 shillings for all municipal employees. Later the Liberal MP for Wolverhampton West until 1945 he exemplified the inextricable link between Wolverhampton and the Manders.

The dedication of the Manders to the affairs of Wolverhampton lasted well into the twentieth century and was matched by that of Sir Alfred Owen to Darlaston, the head of the celebrated Rubery Owen. Back in 1834 a Jabez Rubery had been a gunlock filer, screw turner and gunlock maker in the town. Fifty years later the brothers J. T. and T. W. Rubery had started a factory in Booth Street for making light steel roof work, fencing, gates and the occasional bridge. Later T. W. Rubery left the business and in 1893, his brother went into partnership with Alfred Ernest Owen.

Ernest Owen and John Rubery after joining forces.

A young engineer of talent, foresight and determination, Owen transformed the company. Alert to the rise of new industries and to the potential for supplying them with new products, he oversaw the making of an award-winning chassis frame for a car made from rolled sections and solid round steel bars. In 1910, Owen became sole owner of the company and with his acute vision he added an aviation department, so allowing Rubery Owen to supply small aircraft components in the First World War. By that time, his company was also making car wheels and had taken over Chains Limited of Wednesbury and Nuts and Bolts Ltd of Darlaston – as well as two Birmingham businesses.

Alfred Ernest Owen died in 1929. He was followed ably by his two sons, Sir Alfred and E. W. B. They led a highly skilled, motivated workforce that helped the people of Darlaston withstand the ravages of the Depression of the 1930s and which played a vital role in the Second World War. Rubery Owen's structural department at Darlaston was responsible for building shadow factories, aircraft hangars, Bailey bridges, tank-landing craft and components for the Mulberry Harbours that were so essential to the success of the Normandy Landings. During the same period, the motor-frame department made gun carriages, projectiles, mines and bomb-trolleys; the motor wheel department produced instrument containers, bomb carriers, anti-submarine weapons, bomb tails and much more; whilst the aviation department turned out nuts and bolts for aircraft.

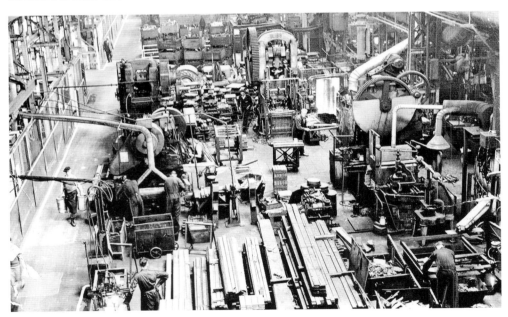

The shop floor of the Rubery Owen factory in its heyday.

After the war Rubery Owen continued to expand, but like all Black Country manufacturers it suffered badly because of the economic problems of the 1970s and unhappily its main plant closed in 1980. The year before the GKN factory had shut down. Just as a century earlier, Darlaston and its people were buffeted by a severe economic downturn. Unfortunately, unlike then, no new industry appeared to provide manufacturing employment.

Thankfully, Rubery Owen Holdings still has a presence locally through Rotech Laboratories and recently it made a gift to the Black Country Living Museum for the Rolfe Street Baths project. Such support for

The works entrance to the historic Rubery Owen factory in Darlaston.

the area builds on the commitment of both Alfred and Owen and his son, Sir Alfred. As early as 1912 the older man provided his workers with a recreation ground with bowling greens and tennis courts. The firm was also one of the first in the Midlands to set up an institute with a canteen, staff dining room, billiards room and reading room and it was a founder member of the Industrial Welfare Society. In the mid-1930s and under the leadership of Sir Alfred, Rubery Owen paid for the refurbishment of the dilapidated old Darlaston graveyard in Cock Street, and added seats to turn it into a garden of rest. Sir Alfred was also a long-term prominent councillor in Darlaston, serving for 37 years until 1974, and was a mayor of the town in 1951.

The commitment of Sir Alfred Owen to Darlaston, of Noah and Benjamin Hingley to Netherton and Dudley, of Reuben Farley to West Bromwich, of Joseph William Sankey to Bilston and of Sir Alfred Hickman and the Manders to Wolverhampton was impressive and salutary. Yes, they did make a lot of money but they could have pulled away from the towns in which they made their wealth and been indifferent to the lives of their workers and their families. They did not do that. They threw themselves into local life and held fast to the concept of civic duty and the ideals of the Civic Gospel. Their example shines brightly as a model still for local involvement by successful businesses.

Chapter 6

BLACK COUNTRY ICONS

Icon is a powerful word. An iconic person is raised up out of the ordinary and made special by their own deeds and by their positive contribution to knowledge or to the well being of society; but an iconic person can also be someone who may not be widely known but whose qualities and character embody those of a people and whose life is emblematic. An iconic person is not necessarily famous but has made a mark and stands out as a positive example.

The Black Country and the district around it have produced a number of iconic figures. In sport, the lamented Duncan Edwards of Dudley had the potential to be one of the greatest footballers in English history. Raised on The Priory, he dreamed of playing for England; but Duncan was no mere dreamer, he was a gifted footballer who knew he had to work hard to make his dreams come true. He did just that. One of the famed 'Busby Babes' Manchester United team of the mid-1950s that gained such accolades for their terrific play, he was capped eighteen times for his country. Killed in the Munich Air Disaster of 1958, Duncan was a footballer who played the game the right way. In his book so aptly entitled *Play Tackle Soccer This Way*, one of the tips he gave to impressionable youngsters was to "always respect the referee and be reasonable at all times".

Duncan Edwards, one of England's finest footballers from Dudley.

Respect and fair play were two of the great qualities of acclaimed tennis player Dorothy Round. Born on Grange Road, Dudley and educated at Dudley Girls' High School, she took to the game from an early age. Talented as she was, Dorothy was eager to learn from her mistakes and to work hard at making her game the best she could. By 1931, she was hitting the headlines and two years later in the Wimbledon final, she faced the great American player, Helen Wills Moody. In an absorbing match, Dorothy showed herself to be a true sportswoman. She won the second set on a controversial line call, but instead of accepting the victory she sportingly argued that her point should be overturned in her opponent's favour. As it was, the call was upheld and Dorothy was given the set – although she went on to lose the match.

That defeat was forgotten in 1934 when Dorothy beat another American, Helen Jacobs, in three sets. The men's singles were won by Fred Perry's and these successes represented the first British 'double' at the championships since 1909. A year later, Dorothy became the first overseas player to win the Australian ladies' singles title and she went on to win Wimbledon again in 1937. Unassuming and eschewing celebrity status, Dorothy was a committed Christian and a Methodist Sunday school teacher.

Modesty was something that also distinguished Jumping' Josie Darby, the champion all round spring jumper of the world who came from Windmill End, Netherton. His speciality was trick jumping and it is recorded that from a standing start he could jump onto the surface of the water in a tank and jump back out again and only wet the soles of his shoes. The holder of word and other records, spring-heeled Josie was the greatest jumper the world had ever known. He appeared before royalty and huge crowds, but "his quiet, easy-going manner devoid of any 'swank' endeared him to all". Josie presented his championship belts to Dudley and after retiring kept the 'Albion' in Dudley. He died in 1937, after having brought to the town through his exploits. Jack Holden did the same for Tipton.

A one-time groundsman at the Palethorpe's sports ground, Jack was regarded by many as the Tiptonian of the twentieth century. He ran for Tipton Harrier and won scores of titles, dominating as he did British distance running before and

Dorothy Round – acclaimed tennis player also from Dudley.

The Tiptonian of the twentieth century – runner Jack Holden.

shortly after the Second World War. In 1950, aged 43, he won the Empire Games marathon in New Zealand and the European Games marathon in Brussels. He was given a civic reception at Tipton Baths following his Empire Games triumph and his deeds are forever recalled in the Jack Holden Gardens near Victoria Park.

One other sportsman stands out as an icon. He was Sydney Francis Barnes. A working-class man from Smethwick, he was a highly talented cricketer at a time when class prejudice stifled the game in England. Sydney could not afford to play day-to-day cricket for little money for Warwickshire and made only four appearances for the county. Instead he worked full time and played League cricket on Saturday afternoons. For four years from 1895 he played in Lancashire, where he gained a high reputation as a bowler.

Sydney Francis Barnes – the best bowler in the world from Smethwick.

Then at the end of 1899, Sydney gained a surprise call up to the England team that was heading for Australia. He justified his selection by taking nineteen wickets in the first two tests, but then broke down with a knee injury.

Despite returning to League cricket and a full-time job, Sydney appeared for England in another 23 test matches up to 1914. In 1908 at Melbourne he took five wickets for 102 runs, and three years later at the same ground he dismissed Australia's top four batsmen in five overs for merely one run. Overall in test cricket Sydney took 189 wickets at an average of 16.43 runs in 27 matches. He was the last man to play test cricket regularly who did not play regular first-class county cricket. Admired by the Australians as the best bowler in the world, Sydney has been placed as fourth in the list of the greatest bowlers in history. He never gained the acclaim he deserved in class-bound England for he was a clerk in a Staffordshire colliery who refused to bend his knee deferentially to the 'gentlemen' of cricket. A self-made man who was proud of his background, Sydney was also a skilled calligrapher and in 1957 he presented Elizabeth II with a scroll of his own work describing the visit of Elizabeth I to Stafford. He died at his home in Chadsmoor, Cannock in 1967.

The Black Country can also claim its literary and film icons. Amongst them is Madeleine Carroll of West Bromwich. Best recalled for her role in the 'Thirty-Nine Steps', she was also a humanitarian who reached out to those in need, especially in the Second World War. Other figures who may be seen as iconic are James Whale, the film director who was born in poverty in Brewery Street, Dudley and went on to make the film 'Frankenstein' in Hollywood in 1931; and Sir Cecil Hardwicke, from The Lye in Worcestershire, who became a celebrated actor. To their number could be added the influential sporting cartoonist, Tom Webster, from Church Street, Bilston, and William Treece.

Treece was born in Wednesbury. Educated at Wednesbury High School for Boys and at Birmingham University, where he read English, history, and Spanish, he found notice as a writer of historical novels for children. Little did I know of his local connection when I used to go to Hudson's Bookshop in New Street, Birmingham and buy his books. It was his trilogy about the Vikings that saw me sail along in longboats with intrepid Norsemen to the riches of distant and exotic Miklagard – Constantinople; and it was his moving work *The Children's Crusade* that I still have on my bookshelves.

Two names stand high as icons who strove to improve society and the lot of their fellow men and women. One came from the edge of the Black Country and did his work on the international stage. The other came to the Black Country and did her work locally. They are Francis Asbury and Sister Dora. Bishop Francis Asbury came from the Newton Road and in the early nineteenth century he went on to evangelise North America for the Methodists by travelling the length and breadth of this exciting new country on the back of a horse. As for Sister Dora, she was born Dorothy Wyndlow Pattison, and though courted by several men she chose work rather than marriage.

In September 1864 she became an Anglican nun and took the name Sister Dora. A year later she was sent to Walsall, where her order provided nurses for the cottage hospital to which victims of industrial accidents were brought. Sister Dora soon came to love both Walsall and its people. She was inspired by the words in Matthew 25: 40, "Inasmuch as ye have done it to the least of

Famous film legend from West Bromwich – Madeleine Carroll.

Francis Asbury from Barr – evangeliser of North America.

these my brethren, ye have done it unto me". Daily she carried out this injunction by selflessly nursing both in-patients and hundreds of out-patients, explaining that "the more I have to do, the stronger and happier I feel".

Soon Sister Dora was indispensable at the hospital not only as a highly skilled surgical nurse but also as a sensitive person who cared for the moral and spiritual welfare of her patients. This was made plain in 1872 when there was a fatal colliery disaster in Pelsall in which 22 men and boys died. Sister Dora could do nothing as a nurse but she headed for Pelsall to comfort the families of the victims at the pithead and to distribute blankets and food.

Three years later Walsall was threatened with a smallpox epidemic and on her own initiative, Sister Dora left the cottage hospital and went to the epidemic hospital for six months to nurse the

Sister Dora in 1873. Beloved by the working-class of Walsall she chose duty before self.

victims. Not long after she was told that she had breast cancer. She carried on with her ministry as long as she could and lived to see the opening of a new hospital in the town. Her family had never understood her calling and when two of her sisters visited her as she faced death she sent them away. She preferred to be nursed by her people, the folk of Walsall. Sister Dora died in Walsall on 24 December 1878. At her funeral, her people mourned her. Her coffin was carried by eighteen railway workers and the whole town turned out to pay its respects. She was buried in Walsall cemetery. Regarded by many as a saint, Sister Dora is still revered in the town she came to love and her people, the working people, paid for a public statue to be put up in her honour.

Lucy Townsend of West Bromwich, Staffordshire was another woman who campaigned for the wellbeing of others. The daughter and wife of vicars of the town, she was an anti-slavery campaigner and the Ladies' Society for the Relief of Negro Slaves was founded at her home in West Bromwich in 1825. It was the first women's anti-slavery society in Britain. Lucy became joint secretary with Mary Lloyd, who was married to Samuel Lloyd. He belonged to the prominent Quaker family that had founded Lloyd's Bank and he owned an iron foundry and colliery at Wednesbury. The couple lived in Wood Green, Wednesbury and their family became best known locally for the company of F. H. Lloyd's in the town.

The society founded by Lucy Townsend and Mary Lloyd was vital in the development of a national network of female anti-slavery societies and had important international connections. It emphasised the sufferings of women under slavery under the motto 'Am I not a woman and a sister?' The two woman were also active closer to home and established the Juvenile Association for West Bromwich and Wednesbury in Aid of Uninstructed Deaf Mutes.

Emma Sproson, née Lloyd, shared Mary Lloyd's name but was not related. Born in 1867 at Pikehelve Street, West Bromwich, she was a remarkable woman. One of seven children, she grew up in poverty because her father, a canal boat builder, was a heavy drinker. In the mid-1870s the family moved to Wolverhampton. Emma had little schooling and from the age of eight was picking coal from the pit bonks and running errands to earn money. When she was just nine, she left home to become a domestic servant for a milk woman. Little Emma cooked, cleaned, and helped her mistress on her evening delivery, although she now attended school four

Emma Sproson – campaigner for the rights of women, from West Bromwich.

days a week. At thirteen, Emma found a full-time job in a shop but was dismissed without a reference when she reported that her mistress's brother had made sexual advances towards her. Unemployed, Emma moved for work to Lancashire, where she began teaching in a Sunday school and joined the church debating society.

During a parliamentary campaign by Lord Curzon she asked him a question. Curzon refused to answer because "she was a woman and did not have the vote". That event pushed Emma to the cause of the suffragettes who were campaigning for adult women to be given the vote. Through hard work she saved enough money to buy a small shop for her and her mom back in Wolverhampton in 1895. After joining the local branch of the Independent Labour Party, she married a fellow member Frank Sproson, who was a postman. In 1906 Emmeline Pankhurst, the founder of the Women's Social and Political Union, stayed at the home of the Sprosons when she came to the town to speak.

The next year Emma was arrested at a suffragette meeting on the green at Westminster Abbey. She was given the option of a twenty shilling fine or fourteen days' imprisonment, and chose the latter. Emma continued to fight for woman's equality and was imprisoned again. After the First World War she focused on local politics and in 1921 was elected councillor for Dunstall ward. She was the first woman councillor in Wolverhampton. Independent of mind and proud of her class, she had fallen out with the middle-class Pankhursts because of their authoritarian approach to the campaign for the suffrage and now she fell out with her fellow councillors when she sought to expose a hospital scandal. Emma lost her seat in 1927 and died nine years later.

There are other Black Country people who deserve to be seen as icons. There's Thomas Attwood of Halesowen, the banker who campaigned for an extension of the vote and who played a vital role in the passage of the Great Reform Act in 1832. There's Arthur Albright of Oldbury, an industrialist and philanthropist, and Richard Juggins of Darlaston, who took a leading part in forming the Nut and Bolt Makers' Association. There's Terry Duffy of Wolverhampton who became president of Amalgamated Union of Engineering Workers; and Don and Roy Richardson, who have powered their Black Country business on to the world stage. Icons they may all be, but all gained from their belonging to the Black Country and all have been sustained by the support of their Black Country fellows.

Lucy Woodall – Chainmaker

The last woman chainmaker in England to make chain by hand, perhaps the last in the world, Lucy held the craft of chainmaking tight to her in her mind, spirit and body. As much as her family and her region, her trade was at the core of her being and Lucy could think no more of putting down her hammer as of putting away her loyalties to kin and place.

Born in Old Hill in 1899, she was one of seven children. When Lucy was little more than ten, the female chainmakers of Cradley, Cradley Heath and Old Hill rose up against their starvation wages and formed a union to fight for their rights. Some employers locked out the women workers. Lucy had vivid memories of these tough and determined women who demonstrated in Cradley Heath wearing their flat caps and shawls and who won their battle for a small rise, for that was better than nothing.

Leaving school when she was thirteen, Lucy went straight into a chain shop in Old Hill at 4 shillings (20p) a week. The hours were long and tiring for a young woman, twelve hours a day Monday to Friday and seven hours on the supposed half day of Saturday when Lucy knocked off at two. Even then there was no relaxing for after work Lucy had to help her Mom black lead the grate and do the shopping.

Lucy Woodall the last women hand chain maker in England. Thanks to Trevor Woodall.

As did every working-class youngster, she handed over her wages to her Mom, receiving back 2d for herself.

After finishing her apprenticeship in 1915, Lucy moved to another chain shop. By now she and her family were living in High Street, Old Hill – today called Highgate Street. She lived there for the rest of her life. After two years she took on another job and then in the early 1920s she settled down with the firm of Harry Stevens in Oak Street, Old Hill. Lucy was to work here for 35 years. For much of this time, she was on 'country work', making chains for agricultural purposes.

In the late 1920s, Lucy met her chap, Jack Woodall, a miner at No. 3 Pit in Netherton. There was no honeymoon, for after their wedding night they both went back to work. Two years later, Lucy had her son, Trevor, and then came disaster: Jack died of pneumonia. Lucy never married again. Loyalty was something ingrained in her. She had one chap and that was Jack. Having left the chain shop to raise Trevor, Lucy went back to Harry Stevens's. It was a hard bed she lay on for Lucy became the breadwinner not only for herself but also for others in her family: "I'd always got so much to do because my sister was here and her was crippled up badly with arthritis. After my sister died it left me with her Beryl (her niece), her Dad and my Mother, besides Trevor to look after".

In 1957, Harry Stevens was bought by Samuel Woodhouse. By now there were few hand-made chainmakers left, but Lucy averred that hand-made chain was better than that which was machined and she stuck to her craft. Year after year she dedicated herself to making chain in the old way, retiring at last at Christmas 1969 – but not for long, for bored without her hammer in her hand she carried on making chain. At last in 1973, Lucy packed up for good, forced into her decision by arthritis. She was 73 years old and had laboured for sixty years and a month. Despite a life of adversity and tough grind, she had no regrets.

Lucy Woodall knew only one way – hard work. And work hard she did. The Black Country should be proud of her and her kind. Little money did they gain for their endeavours and little money did they seek. They asked not for financial rewards but for food on the table, companions to chat with and family to care for. We, their people, owe it to them to pass on to those yet to come the dignity, the fortitude and the independent spirit of the likes of Lucy Woodall.

William Perry – The Tipton Slasher

Born in 1819, Bill Perry was the son of a boatee from Tipton. From when he was seven worked on the cut helping his father to take night soil from the town into the countryside. It was a dirty, stinking and vile job fetching away the mess of cess pits and closets, but poor families like the Perrys had no choice. They had to collar or be clammed. Hungry days there were and days a many without proper food – so much so that Bill was ravaged by rickets, the deficiency of Vitamin D that softens the bones. This bent his left leg to such an angle that he was called K Legs.

Disabled and with no schooling, Bill Perry went on to make his mark. At twelve he tipped six feet tall and was feared as a hard and relentless bare-fisted fighter. Soon he gained the nickname of the Tipton Slasher – because he fought with round right-arm blows in a slashing motion. Praised as the Tiptonian Hercules, he beat all comers and then went to London to really make his name. He challenged all the best fighters in England to take him on. Few dared and from 1851 Bill Perry was acclaimed as the champion of all England. With no challengers he retired to keep the 'Champion of England' beer house in Spon Lane, West Bromwich.

Then in 1857 he was challenged by the smaller but younger Tom Sayers. Bill was 38, sixteen stone and badly out of shape but he risked everything. He was cut to pieces but still the Slasher would not ask for barley. For almost two hours he was punished by Sayers. At last, his backers stopped the fight but blinded by his own blood, the Tipton Slasher had to be held down by his four seconds whilst the sponge was thrown in.

The statue of William Perry the Tipton Slasher in Tipton.

Bill Perry returned to the boats and shifting night soil. He worked hard and eventually bought his own house in Gibbett Lane, Bilston. A good husband and father, Bill Perry died on Christmas Eve 1880 in his own home. He was the last of his kind:

And Perry bold of Tipton town, all bone and muscled meat,
Who smiling comes up to the scratch on firmly planted feet,
And moving forwards fights and fights and cannot brook retreat,
When he is gone the Prize Ring goes 'twill die in his defeat.
The last old English pugilist,
One of the olden time.

(From the 'Fine Old English Pugilist').

Bill Perry was a hard man in a hard age, but his heart was never hardened and nor was his soul. He never knew what it was to give in, and he was a man who never cheated and who never forgot where he came from. He is a man of whom the Black Country is rightly proud. The undaunted Bill Perry, the Tipton Slasher.

Henry Fowler – Political Campaigner

Henry Hartley Fowler was firm of purpose and tenacious in achieving his aims. The son of a Methodist minister from the north of England, from a young age he was steadfast in his determination to make something of himself – and make something of himself he did for he became a mayor of Wolverhampton, a Member of Parliament for the town, a freeman of the borough, a politician of national standing who held high office, and the first Lord Wolverhampton. His rise was spectacular and it owed much not only to his own endeavours but to his marriage in 1857 to Ellen Thorneycroft, the daughter of the biggest employer in Wolverhampton at the Shrubbery Ironworks in Horseley Fields.

Henry was a young man in a hurry to do good and in 1858 he became a local councillor. A decade and more before Joseph Chamberlain gained such a reputation in Birmingham for promoting municipal socialism, Henry Fowler began to press for Wolverhampton to provide better facilities for its citizens. A man of deep Christian belief who worshipped first at Darlington Street Methodist Church and then at Trinity Methodist Church on the Compton Road, his Christianity informed and underpinned his humanitarian concern and his involvement in the public health movement.

In particular, he was keen to push forward a proper system of drainage and sewerage. This was needed badly. In 1848, Robert Rawlinson had inquired into the public health of the town and had reported unfavourably. He came upon "disgustingly filthy" privies that were unfit for use; in the Caribee Island neighbourhood he found "ruinous cottages'" with no drains or sewers or even a water supply; and in Canal Street he found "middens, pig-sties, and open stagnant ditches which were a great nuisance to the place, and might be cheaply drained".

In spite of this damning inquiry, little action was taken. Fowler was disgusted by the 'spend-

Sir Henry Fowler, later Lord Wolverhampton.

as-little party'. His call to action was as compelling as it was devastating, declaring that "the sewerage is a public necessity; it is the disgrace of the Town Council that the necessity has existed so long; it will be their crime if it exists any longer". Fowler and his supporters won the day and in 1863 a drainage and sewerage scheme was authorised for Wolverhampton. Six years later he succeeded in persuading the council to bring in a fresh supply of water which was then pumped in from Cosford.

A staunch Liberal, Henry Fowler believed in the importance of local government and in equal laws, equal rights and equal privileges for all, irrespective of their class or creed. His tenacity and talent led to him becoming mayor of Wolverhampton in 1862 and then MP for the town in 1880. Twelve years later the municipality recognised his standing when he became the first freeman of the Borough. As ever, Fowler was modest of himself and generous to others. He stated that "in the service of this Corporation I learnt lessons of the administration of public affairs, the transaction of public business, and of the management of public finance which have been of inestimable value to me in various positions which I have been called upon to hold".

Two years later, in a short-lived Liberal Government, Fowler was appointed President of the Local Government Board. It was a fitting appointment for a man so convinced of the value of local government and of the need to break the power of the gentry in the countryside. His most important measure was the Local Government Act of 1894 which facilitated the establishment of parish, district and county councils.

The Liberals soon after lost power but returned to office in 1906. Despite his age of 76, Sir Henry was made Chancellor of the Duchy of Lancaster. Two years later he moved to the House of Lords when he became a viscount. He took the title of Lord Wolverhampton and was the first Methodist to be made a peer. Despite ill health, Lord Fowler was appointed to the position of Lord President of the Privy Council. He had to resign in June 1910 because of his growing physical weakness. Sadly on 6 January 1911 his beloved wife, Ellen, died. Lord Fowler was overcome with grief. He died weeks later.

Henry Fowler embodied the qualities of the people and town of Wolverhampton. An incomer, he had embraced Wolverhampton and Wolverhampton had embraced him. Steadfast, persevering, hard working, loyal, liberal, democratic, moral and determined, his endeavours and talents ensured that Wolverhampton had a seat at the big table in London. His like had not been seen before in the town and it may be that his like will not be seen again. He strove to create a better society and his beliefs call out to us still. He was a man of compassion and morality, a politician of the highest principles, and a Wulfrunian of whom Wolverhampton should be as proud now as it was then.

Pat Collins – King of the Showmen

Pat Collins was the showman of England and he achieved all that he did in England from Bloxwich. His favourite saying was, "We only pass this way once – Let us do what we can when we can", and he did all that he could and more. Born in Cheshire, from the age of ten Pat went with his father taking simple rides around the fairs of the north west. As a young men he branched out on his own and claimed to have started with "two doll stalls and a set of swings". Then in 1882 and still in his early twenties, he and his first wife, Flora, in 1882 settled Shaw's Leasowe, in The Birchills, Walsall. He made a living from rides on steam horses on wasteland off Bradford Street, where the Arcade now stands, and at Bloxwich Wakes.

Building up his business, Collins to travel to the wakes that each Black Country held and took on the fairs at Oldbury, Darlaston and Walsall. In 1889 he was involved in the setting up of the Van Dweller's and Showmen's Protection Society, later the Showmen's Guild (Allen and Williams). By then he owned several roundabouts, including two sets of three-abreast galloping horses and a switchback roundabout. The next year he leased the ground on which Birmingham's Onion Fair was held. This was at the Old Pleck in Aston. Unfortunately the showmen were preyed on by the Black Mask Gang and Peaky Blinders who asked protection money of 2s 6d or 5s (25p) per ride.

Years later Collins was angered when it was reported that he and his men had used knuckle dusters to beat the gangs away. He did not do so. As he wrote to the Showmen's Guild, he approached Inspector McManus for police protection. McManus was famed for his toughness but even he was taken aback when Collins asked him for police protection. Nevertheless, McManus agreed to help Collins. Collins recalled that the gangsters came down with:

> One big fellow with two big scars on his face and cauliflower ears, then the police came into action; the old inspector used the real old Irish kick on this ruffian and no sooner he was put down away they went for their life and he told all the others what had happened. An hour later down comes the Peaky Blinders, the police of course were waiting for them also, and they got the same dose, but believe me there was no fighting or knuckle dusters used and it is simply a pack of lies.

Pat Collins's fortunes waxed and he became the leading showman in England. So successful was he that in 1899 he floated it as a limited company with a capital of £40,000. The firm's assets included a top motion galloping horse machine, mountain ponies, an ostrich Machine, two living wagons, and a menagerie. By this time, he had also purchased both new and second-hand steam road locomotives to power his rides.

Clever and innovative, Collins embraced new technology to make fairgrounds even more appealing at a time when they were the only form of holiday for most working-class people, and he grasped hold of the potential of the nascent film industry. In 1900 at Bloxwich Wakes he presented moving pictures in his cinematograph show. He went on to travel with at least five bioscope shows. The finest was the second Wonderland show, which was custom-built and featured a huge 112-key Marenghi organ that used 5,000 lights and 14 arc lamps.

Collins's stopped travelling this show by 1914 and moved into the cinema business. By the mid-1920s his firm had thirteen cinemas, including three in the Black Country. One of these was the grand 'Grosvenor' in Bloxwich. He also owned the Waldorf Skating Ring in Birmingham and was still involved in running as many as four fairs a week.

Pat Collins and his wife, Clara, at Walsall Town Hall in 1923.

Unsurprisingly for a man who did so much for show people, Collins was elected president of the Showmen's Guild of Great Britain in 1909. He held the position for twenty years and was the longest-serving president in the guild's history. He was also active in the public life of Walsall. A councillor for Birchills Ward from 1918, four years later he was elected Liberal MP. He was defeated in 1924 but continued to serve the borough as a councillor and became an alderman in 1930.

Elected mayor of Walsall in 1938 and made a Freeman of the borough a year afterwards, it is said that Collins refused a knighthood because he had been born plain Pat Collins and would die the same. He did so in 1943 at his home, Lime Tree House, High Street, Bloxwich – next door to which the wakes were held. That site is now a supermarket car park. Showland had indeed lost its Grand Old Man and so had Walsall and Bloxwich. Powered by traction engine generators, such extravaganzas made Pat's fairs popular and successful nationwide, as well as at Bloxwich Wakes, and even on a permanent site in Sutton Park from 1917.

Pat Collins eagerly embraced new technology for his fairground attractions.

Chapter 7

UNIVERSITY OF HARD KNOCKS: SAM'S STORY

How many times have you heard someone say, "I could write a book"? And how often has someone breviting around into their family's past wished that some distant ancestor had done just that, put it all down and breathed life into the stark names of kin listed in the registers of births, deaths and marriages. Each and everyone of us does indeed have a story to tell, a story that embraces not only our own life but also the lives of those bonded to us by blood, friendship and acquaintance. Each and everyone of us could and should write down all that we have heard, seen, felt and experienced. But the assertion that we could do so is seldom followed by the action of writing. For so many of us, we are pushed away from bringing out the book of our life by pressures of home, work and a variety of involvements, so that we leave the publication in our minds where only we can see it.

The person who actually does write it all down is rare. But for all that they are exceptional they are not part of an elite that is separated from the mass of us, rather they reach out to all of us through the commonality of their experiences and the sharing of them with us. We identify with their childhood games and scrapes, we see our moms and dads and nans and grandads in their descriptions of their relatives, we feel their rush of joy as they recall their courtships and happy days, we taste with them the bitterness of hard times, we hark alongside them at the sounds of factory bulls and wheels on cobbles, and we smell as much as they do the acrid air of industry mingling with the tantalising whiff of fresh bread.

Each major city and region has its autobiographers who have brought to the fore the working people whence they sprang and to whom they belonged. Salford holds up Robert Roberts, the son of a skilled worker and a shopkeeper who wrote the *Classic Slum* and who intuitively identified that "every industrial city, of course, folds within itself a clutter of loosely defined overlapping 'villages'" that were almost self-contained communities.

The North East is fortunate in having Catherine Cookson, not only a novelist of note but also the author of *Our Kate*, in which she shuns sentimentality to make plain the tough bed upon which slept the poor of East Jarrow – the poor like her mother who "worked for anybody and everybody". As for the East End of London, it can look to the recollections of Arthur Harding brought together in *East End Underworld*, which highlights the thrill of the local shopping street, in his case Church Street in the Old Nichol – "the high heaven of everything in the district".

In the West Midlands, Birmingham is the richer for the memories of Kathleen Dayus, whose first book *Her People* did just that, shed light on her folk, those who had been forgotten by so many historians. One day she found herself walking down the old end, that part of Hockley where she had grown up, and it struck her how different it was to when she had lived there. Then it was so crammed with humanity it was more like a rabbit warren and "the poor people who struggled to live there until that struggle killed them were my people". Those people may have had nothing but Kathleen averred that they didn't deserve to be forgotten: "My people; my parents and their friends and my brothers and sisters and the rest of us who fought for a crust here ought to be remembered".

The Black Country, too, has its small yet vital group of life story writers who have striven to remember their people. Harold Parsons is foremost amongst them. Widely admired for his work as a writer and editor of the *Blackcountryman* magazine, he penned *Substance and Shadow* in 1982. It told of how he was raised in Salop Street, Dudley, "a lively self-contained community, with almost every kind of retail shop imaginable between Eve Hill and Shavers End, all drawing custom from the streets of working-class houses which clustered in the area where tower blocks stand today". The family lived above and behind the shop, and their back room "looked out over the party yard, the light partly blocked out by the brewhouse. For years I gazed out on cobbles and dirt, and the neighbour's fowl ranging free".

Harold's book is sensitive, thoughtful and descriptive, allowing us to understand with him the longstanding difficulties faced by his stoical mother, the disappointments that marred his father's life, the spiritualism of his Aunt Mary and the characteristics of his workmates at Baylis's, like cheerful Percy Hope, known as Pears Soap, who used to visit his allotment before coming to work. Throughout the book, the people of the Black Country stand out, proud, phlegmatic, and made distinctive by their dry sense of humour and a rich dialect.

These features are as powerful in the unpublished life story of Sam Humphries. He has done what all of us should do – written down his memories. His unpublished life story is a fascinating account and also draws in the lives of those dear to him. Above all, it brings to the fore the dangers of working life – but, crucially, it also brings out the stoicism of working-class folk and how they strove to make their bed as best they could, no matter how hard it was. Below are extracts from Sam's story:

I was born into a working class family, the seventh son of Joseph and Annie Humphries nee Timmins at a little house, number 44 Hollybush Street, Cradley Heath in the county of Staffordshire. There were eight of us males and one sister,

Annie junior, cramped into this little box of a house. These were the survivors, as there were some losses including my brother Wilfred who drowned in the Severn at Stourport. I remember my brother Wilfred's preparation for his August bank holiday camping holiday at Stourport with his mate, a man named Tommy Crampton who lived about four doors away from my family. I was told by one of my brothers (I think it was Tom), that some of the last words my father said to Wilf and "doh thee bloody come back drownded". As fate would have it, this is precisely what happened.

They also suffered the loss of my baby sister Marion who was the apple of their eye. I remember playing with her with my brother Arthur when she was seriously ill, but I did not realise how serious the situation was as I could only have been about six or seven years old. My sister Annie recalls that as she was setting out for work (she worked in Birmingham Jewellery Quarter at the time), Marion pleaded to her, "Annie, give me a love". When she got home that day, they had to tell her that sadly little Marion had died. I remember only one funeral, when I had to go over to stay with one of mother's friends on the other side of the road. I saw the hearse which was drawn in those days by black horses. I do not remember if it was Wilf or Marion. I hope to be forgiven for using an old saying, but my parents were educated at the "University of

A trip to the Festival of Britain. Sam is bottom right, and also on the photo are his brothers Abe, Tom and George, nephew John (on lap), Jack Horton, Harold Ward, Harry Wragg, Kenny Homer, Alan Cole and Wes Tilley. Photos courtesy of Sam Humphries.

Hard Knocks" as were many good people in those poor, downtrodden areas of the Black Country as it was known.

My older brothers were working in the drop forging industry, the trade to which nearly all of us, including myself and also my sister Ann, were to spend most of our working lives. I was always a very strong person, which I found out when I went to Lomey Town School in Cradley Heath. In the Science Room where Mr. Lawson Cornock of Coxes Lane was Science Teacher, was a weight shaped like a bell with a ring on the top. I was not very big at the time, at eleven years old, but I could pick up the weight by using my little finger through the ring and only one other boy could do this, his name was Derek Penn and his father kept a butcher's shop in Cradley Heath, Bank Street. He was a much bigger lad than me.

When I got older I could bend six inch nails with my bare hands, and if you thinks that's easy – try it. I could still do this after losing the ring finger from my right hand. Another feat which I used to do when I was about eighteen was to pick up a workmate. He was fourteen stone, and I picked him right up to shoulder height. I could also wrap my arm around his waist and hold him under my arm. His name was Stanley Stokes and we worked together for many years without ever falling out. It was a fine example of men working together to both our advantage to put food in the mouths of our families.

I suffered a very serious accident at work one Friday night. I was working on the afternoon shift, 2pm – 10pm. I think my father was in the factory at the time. It was caused by the rope (which tied the belt to the forge hammer which I was operating) breaking. This caused the operating lever that I used to control the hammer to come up and hit my face beneath my right ear with such force that it ruptured a blood vessel in my head. I was taken by my boss, Mr. Ron Hadley, in his Morris 8 to Dudley Guest Hospital, Princess Elizabeth or it could have been Queen Elizabeth Ward, in a bed over which was a plaque telling all and sundry that the bed was donated by The Miners' Welfare. I think I probably looked very much like a miner after a few hours in Thomas Price's dirty stamp shop.

I was tested for nerve reaction by sticking needles in my body in various places, but according to bystanders from my family, there was no reaction at all. My memory was also gone and I did not remember getting my wages that night. The doctor's verdict was that if I survived the next five hours I would be lucky owing to the vast amount of blood which I had lost. Being an extremely fit young man, I did survive even though there was very little hope even several days later. I walked out of the hospital eight days later and was brought home in the same Morris 8 that I was taken in.

This is what I meant when I spoke of my parents being educated at the university of hard knocks. Another very trying time for my parents was when my oldest brother George was blown off a factory roof where he was carrying out

This photo includes Sam's mom Annie (nee Woodall) on front, Lily Woodall, Aunt Rita Green, Kathy Woodall, Florrie and his dad (Joseph)

erection work for someone who was to become my eventual boss, Mr. Fred Allan. He suffered two broken wrists and fractured skull and was on the danger list for quite some time. If you add all these happenings to my own accident and also the loss of other children before I was born, you realise how my parents suffered some hard times. The fact that they loved their family I have no doubts whatsoever. This, I think, is why I also love all my children, one no less or more than any other …

I seem to remember there was much more contrast between the seasons in those times. I remember long hot summers and cold winters. I recall my father sending me down to Hardy's shop which was about six doors away from our house to fetch a pint of beer which cost either threepence or fourpence depending on mild or bitter beer. We had quite a heavy fall of snow, with drifting in the gutters. I fell down and completely disappeared in the snowdrift. The first frost began in September, this was always evident because our mother used to take us hop-picking which used to serve as a holiday. There was frost on the hops when we used to go down to the hop-fields about 7 o'clock in the morning.

These were lovely times for my brothers and myself. The times at Newnam Bridge and at Lower Court Farm, Ullinswick near Bromyard, I will always remember with affection. I remember my brother Arthur and myself were taken ill at Ullinswick with sore throats and the district nurse came from Knightwick to examine us. She was named Nurse Stainer and she had us isolated because she thought we may have caught diphtheria. It turned out it was only tonsillitis, but the funny part was that the only place the farmer could find for us away from the other kids was right next to Farmer Harmer's bull pen. We could see him and hear him all day and all night for to us he was a monstrous beast...

I will devote some time here to how I met my wife Lillian. I was not attached to any one as I had broken off with my girlfriend of some two years and was at a loose end. I made friends with Georgie Wood, Derek Woodhouse and Peter Round and we started going to a skating rink in Dudley called the Gliderdrome. This is the place where I was to meet my girlfriend who became my wife. Lillian Laura Arnold was helping out behind the refreshment bar with her friend Doris Evans. She was only about sixteen at this time and had come over from Londonderry, Northern Ireland when she was twelve years old.

The worst winter I remember was in 1947 when the whole country was covered with a blanket of snow and ice. I had been courting my future wife for some months

Sam with wife Lil and children Pam, Eileen and Clive at Toys Lane.

when the winter of 1946 going into 1947 brought almost everything to a standstill. We had to shut down most of industry as no fuel was available to operate the power stations. We could not buy any coal for our fires. We found out that men were digging low quality coal out of the old pit banks at Saltwell Coppice which is now a nature reserve.

I think at this time by brother Arthur was in Italy doing his national service as a truck driver in the Service Corps. My other brothers and myself went and joined these people digging coal out of the pit banks. Some of the men stayed in the holes they had dug all day and all night working by candle-light when it got dark so that no one could take over their holes. I don't remember if we followed this routine, but I know it was a dangerous game. I think what may have prevented the trenches collapsing was that the ground was that hardened by the continual frost that it was like stone. I also remember going up to Bath Street to visit Lil, and her father George had to cut a tunnel down to the outside toilet through the snow as it was up to the roof the toilet. There were no inside toilets for ordinary people in those days. The winter altogether must have lasted all of five months and seemed never ending.

In my early years where I was born we had some good neighbours, my Aunt who was my mother's half-sister, lived next door with my grandmother. She was eventually married to a Mr. Ted Green who came from Cradley. Next door to my grandmother lived the Whittles, whose daughter Irene was a friend of my sister. Next door there was the Homers whose family ran in parallel with my own. The older sisters were close to my older family members, the younger boys were the same ages as myself, Abe, John and Arthur, so we were mated up with our neighbours children by our different ages.

None of our neighbours were wealthy but they helped each other in times of need. One of my friends, Billy Lloyd, lived at the pub, "The Hand of Providence" which was at the upper part of Hollybush Street. Billy's mom used to pay for me to go with him to the cinema which was quite a treat for me. Eventually Billy and his parents went to live at Holly Hall near Dudley.

My mother and father both made chain and I feel that my mother must have given up a great deal when she married my father because she obviously came from a good home, a fact which I think is evident when you look at her portrait photographs. I will recount here a funny story which I was told by my sister regarding my parents. At the time they worked in a chain shop which was situated on the yard of their house and was only about four yards from the back door, across from what was known as the fode. It consisted of a paved area between the house and the chainshop.

Anyway, getting back to the story – it seems my mother and father had been in bed for some time when my mother woke up and became alarmed as it seemed like broad daylight. She immediately nudged my father and said to him "Joe, get up, we've overlay ourselves". Which in plain English – "we have overslept". They got up right away, dressed and went into the chainshop to start work. They did a full day's work which meant they turned a certain quantity of rods of iron into chain. Then they found out it was not the sun that was shining when they woke but a very large, brightly shinning full moon, which meant they had done a full day's work, had gone to bed for what must have been about three hours or less and done another full day's work. I can understand this happening as I remember the chainshop. It had no windows to speak of and the door was the only place light could have got in and was in two parts. Once they had started work they probably would not notice any changes in the light.

I will now write of my years in Providence Methodist Church Choir. I think I was in for about sixteen years all told and they were very happy, rewarding times for me. Betty Morris was the choir mistress and she was an excellent leader. She also arranged the anniversary with her husband, Tony, who was the church superintendent. I took part in nearly every concert and anniversary and they were lovely occasions. I actually got some solo parts in some of the cantatas and anthems and the choir always told me how well I coped. There were three of us from the male voice choir in Providence – myself and Harry and Don Yates. Over the years in both choirs, I formed friendships with as many people as I did in the police. I also helped out with other choirs on special occasions, these included High Town Ragged, Overend Methodist, Cradley Trinity and Cradley St Peter's. I sang with St. Peter's Choir in the St Martin's Church in Birmingham Bullring, but I think the

Sam (left) with Jack Jones (centre) and a chap called Arthur at Thomas Price, the Eagle Works. The firm's office was in Meredith Street. And the drop forge was in Hollybush Street.

most ambitious concert I was on was with Cradley Heath Male Voice and this was in Wellingborough Cathedral.

I would like to tell you here how my father and mother helped the war effort, when he was called upon by my old boss, Mr. Fred Allan, to make hand-forged iron rings for the Admiralty. These rings were around three to four inches in diameter and as my father used be a chainmaker by trade, it was not too difficult to make the rings. When he had finished joining the ends forming the rings, it was necessary to drive what is known as a mandril through the ring. This was a piece of steel made on a turning lathe and was tapered to where the largest part of the steel was the size of the inside diameter of the ring. The mandril had to be forced through the ring while it was still hot and this was done with the use of a small sledge hammer.

When my mother was not busy in the home, she would go to my father's forge which was situated in our own backyard and she would help by wielding the sledgehammer to drive the forming mandril through the rings. As any steel specialist will tell you, steel becomes crystallised by continuous hammering and then can be dangerous. On one occasion, a fragment flew off either the hammer head or the mandril, probably through my mother's mis-striking. It penetrated my father's leg, passing first through the cloth of his trousers and went so deep that the hospital told him it would have to remain there for the rest of his life.

As fate would have it, I had a similar accident at Price's. My brother Arthur was knocking one of the wedges (which we always called keys) into the hammer when I felt a very violent pain in my hand. I don't think I have ever fainted in my life, but I came very close on this occasion.

The fact is I have one finger smashed in one incident and a very severe wound to my leg in another, but never even felt faint. I was told the object striking the bone in my hand with such force caused the fainting feeling. I had to go in to hospital to have the piece removed about two weeks later. As the Humphries clan never had time off, I continued to work till I went to have the piece removed and was told I should not have carried on working as the pressure I exerted while stamping could have caused the sharp edge of the metal to sever a nerve in my hand. I could have lost the use of my hand just by doing my normal every-day job.

I don't think we appreciate the heartache we bring to our parents till we, ourselves become parents. I know some of the things we did would be heartbreaking if done by my own kids. When you travel down this long road called life, sometimes the road is broad and bathed in sunshine, and other times it is very narrow, boulder strewn with many pitfalls. But a life that was either one or the other would be very bland and may be even boring. How can you know a very happy day if you never knew a sad one? Life is composed of all kinds of days and the sad or bad days are a test of an individual's character in the face of joy or adversity. Life is not a bed of roses and death is the final equaliser. So live for today in the best way you can.

Chapter 8

PROVIDENCE METHODIST CHURCH
COLLEY GATE

Providence City in Providence County, New England in the United States of America: the capital and largest city in Rhode Island – what connection could it have with the Black Country? A powerful one, if we believe in the importance of place names, for Providence City shares its meaning with the Providence Church in Colley Gate in Cradley. With a population of just over 1.6 million in the Providence metropolitan district, it is one of the largest such areas in the States. The four Black Country boroughs of Dudley, Sandwell, Walsall and Wolverhampton together with South Staffordshire and Cannock Chase have about 400,000 fewer citizens, but they also belong to a major conurbation – and just as Providence USA was once proclaimed as the Beehive of Industry so too was the Black Country a hive of manufacturing endeavour. So if there are similarities between the two regions in their size in and in their affinity to the making of things, what then does Providence mean?

Providence was founded by Roger Williams, a Puritan minister who arrived in Boston in 1631 – a decade after the Pilgrim Fathers had made their way to what they

would call New England. During his ministry in Salem and Plymouth he disagreed vehemently with the authorities in the new colony of Massachusetts. About to be sent back to face trial in England, he fled the new settlements with a small band of brothers. A staunch advocate of the belief that the Native Americans were the equals of settlers, he had become friendly with the local tribes and went about from one to another. He later remembered that "I was sorely tossed for one fourteen weeks, in a bitter winter season, not knowing what bread or bed did mean". Eventually he happened

Inside the 1856 chapel. Notice the gas lighting. I thank Derek Trickett for his help in sourcing these photos and for his kindness in providing a history of the Providence Chapel.

upon the site of Providence with twelve "loving friends and neighbours". He called it so because of "God's merciful Providence" in taking care of him and leading him to find the place. In the ensuing years there arose a major town, whose people were passionately attached to cause of the liberty of conscience.

The Methodist church in Colley Gate was also called Providence by devout men and women who held fast to the conviction that God was wise and cared for and guided humanity. Derived from a Latin word meaning foresight, the belief in Providence is made plain in the Bible by Psalm 127, one of those by Solomon. Also known as "A Pilgrim Psalm" it declares that unless God "builds the house, they who build it labour in vain", unless God "protects the city, the watchmen awake in vain". The founders of Providence in Colley Gate harked well to that injunction and built their house with God's grace and under His direction.

Lying on the road from The Lye to Halesowen, Colley Gate was originally a small gathering of people in the hamlet of Cradley but as Cradley industrialised so too did Colley Gate – and so sure as manufacturing grew so too did Methodism strike deep into the souls of the local workers. Its charismatic founder, John Wesley, was himself deeply attached to the concept of providence. After he escaped safely from the mobs that had captured him and dragged him about Wednesbury and Walsall in 1743, he wrote in his *Journal* that "I never saw such a chain of providences before, so many convincing proofs that the hand of God is on every person and thing and overruling all as it seemeth Him good".

Wesley returned to the Black Country several times, receiving more friendly and neighbourly receptions and gaining many adherents – although he still had enemies. On Tuesday 24 October 1749 he came to Dudley:

At one I went to the market place, and proclaimed the name of the Lord to a huge, unwieldy, noisy multitude; the greater part of them seemed in no wise to know "wherefore they were come together." I continued speaking about half an hour, and many grew serious and attentive, till some of Satan's servants pressed in, raging and blaspheming, and throwing whatever came to hand. I then retired to the house from which I came.

The multitude poured after and covered over with dirt many that were near me; but I had only a few specks. I preached in Wednesbury at four, to a nobler people, and was greatly comforted among them; so I was likewise in the morning, Wednesday, 25. How does a praying congregation strengthen the preacher.

In 1761, Wesley came back to Dudley, preaching to a large and quiet congregation, leading him to comment that "the scene is changed since the dirt and stones of this town were flying about me on every side". Three years later he rode to Dudley again, emphasising that "formerly a den of lions" it was now quiet, and his local supporters "had just finished their preaching-house, which was thoroughly filled. I saw no trifler, but many in tears".

It would seem likely that the crowds who harked to Wesley's message in Dudley included folk from nearby places like Cradley. Certainly by 1766 a Wesleyan Methodist Society had been formed there, and within two years a small chapel had been put up in Butcher's Lane. It was just 30 foot long and 20 foot broad. Then on Monday 19 March 1766, on his way through Staffordshire to Manchester, this clergyman who reached out so mightily to the poor, the marginalised, the outcast and the forgotten came to Cradley itself. He preached at the Dungeon Head on the High Street, near to the site of the Baptist Chapel. The stone upon which he stood is now at High Town Ragged School.

Wesley wrote that "I rode to Cradley (from Wednesbury). Here also the multitude obliged me to stand abroad, although the north wind whistled about my head. About one I took the field to Stourbridge. Many of the hearers were as wild as colts untamed; but the bridle was in their mouths. At six I began in Dudley. The air was as cold as I had almost ever felt, but I trust God warmed many hearts."

The visit of Wesley must have given a boost to the local Wesleyans, but in 1786 their chapel in Butcher's Lane was sold and for the next decade they met at a house in Dungeon Head. Then in 1796 they bought the old Presbyterian Meeting House. It would seem that the Methodists of Colley Gate came into Cradley to worship, but in the mid-nineteenth century a move was made towards an independent meeting place. In his history of Providence Church published in 1956, Fred Willetts explained that:

> among the many folk of strong character who had been influenced by the Methodist movement were Mr and Mrs. Benjamin Oliver of Clows Top near Bewdley.
>
> They came to live in the area we know as the Slad Piece. Mrs. Oliver was an enthusiastic Wesleyan and she made it her particular business to start a Church in Colley Gate. Probably before that, there was in existence some kind of Society and meeting places, because in the vestry there is a plan dated 1838 which shows preachers planned at Colley Gate, but there is no record of a meeting place.

Mrs. Oliver started meetings in her own home in Barracks Lane. Obviously for some time meetings were held there weekly and possibly prayer meetings in mid-week. As the membership of the meeting grew, the worshippers moved into the clubroom at the back of the 'White Lion', Colley Gate, (now the 'Little Chop House'). This room was over some stables and "frequently the parson at that time a man named Butterworth was known to pray 'to be delivered from the discomfort and close proximity of horses, cows, pigs and poultry'." Thence the Colley Gate Methodists took themselves to an old malthouse in Windmill Hill, just below the

Inside the 1886 building, now used as a carpenter's shop.

'White Lion'. This was on the main road between Stourbridge and Halesowen, along which were toll gates. Nearby, "Spring Lane or Furlong Lane as we know it today was a narrow country lane with fields either side for the most part".

No records of that time remain, but the site of the old chapel was part of a field belonging to Thomas Brookes of Lye Waste, and Colley Orchard was probably a footpath. Then in about 1854 eight dedicated men decided to form a Trust, collect money from themselves and friends, and purchase the spot. Within a year or so they achieved their objective and 28 October 1856 the 347 square yards on the lower corner of Colley Orchard and Windmill Hill was sold to the Trust for the sum of £60 14s. 6d.

Fred Willetts affirmed that "we must realise and acknowledge the great sacrifice of these eight men – the pioneers who raised the first Chapel. It can only be described as a miracle of faith and perseverance". Their names were Thomas Cox, John Priest, Edward Harris, Peter Boxley, Samuel Bache, Samuel Wyre, Joseph Moore, and Thomas Pearson. Three of them could not write their own names and signed the legal documents with a cross.

Mr and Mrs Oliver were strong supporters of the move and generously gave £20 towards the building of the church. In his fascinating and informed history, Fred Willetts records that "only £2 of that money was ever repaid the remainder was eventually forgiven. The late John Oliver was a nephew of Mr. and Mrs. Benjamin Oliver and he married the daughter of Edward Harris, one of the first Trustees. They remained lifelong members of the Church. John Oliver died in 1934."

Samuel Wyre, another of the eight Trustees, had a close friend named Samuel Ellesmore. He was a carpenter who lived in Two Gates and according to chapel tradition he did all the woodwork. The square, brick building with cast-iron warehouse windows held about 50 people at a push. It cost around £300 to build and although built in 1856 was formally opened on 5 April 1857.

It is presumed that the church was named Providence by the founders. Immediately it became associated with the Stourbridge circuit of the Methodist New Connexion. This had broken from Wesleyan Methodism in 1797 because of a dispute about the position and rights of the laity. Influenced by Alexander Kilham, the New Connexion adherents believed that the Wesleyans gave too much power to the ministers and so decided that at their conferences, ministers and laymen were to be of equal number. The laymen themselves were chosen by the circuits. The first circuit Minister for Providence was the Reverend W. Reynolds, whilst the first sermon preached in the new building was by Mr. Simon of Dudley Circuit.

Providence Church was heated by a large closed-in stove in the middle, around which were four high-backed seats. That was the extent of the seating. Artificial lighting later came via primitive gas jets. The preacher stood in a pulpit that: "was very much like a cupboard in shape and placed against the back wall of the Chapel". Sunday School services for children were held in the church but at different times.

Fred Willetts records that the months following the opening must have been "a very trying period. People were poor; wages varied between a few shillings and a pound per week, and the cost of living was relatively high." Just to keep the chapel going a mortgage for £150 had to be raised soon after worship had begun, and this was a debt that was not repaid for well over twenty years. Despite their trials and tribulations the faithful of Providence devoted their Sundays to worship, as enjoined to do so in the Bible.

At seven in the morning they met for an hour's prayer meeting; from nine till ten thirty they worked with the Sunday School, after which there was preaching, singing and worshipping until twelve noon. Following dinner there was another Sunday School for an hour from one thirty, which led into the Divine Service that lasted until four. After another short gap, at five thirty came missioning to the district and inviting

A Sunday School Anniversary 1950s.

99

people to chapel. This lasted thirty minutes and preceded another Divine Service until seven thirty, after which came one more prayer meeting of half an hour. Finally, the members of the meeting went to visit sick and pray with them.

The history of Fred Willetts brings to life the fervour of these early Methodists. He mentions that:

> so enthusiastic were some of these old pilgrims that one of the local preachers, Higgins by name, walked all the way from Kidderminster, returning there on foot after preaching all day. Samuel Jones was a locomotive engine driver at Corngreaves Works. Each week-end he had to wash out the tubes and boilers of his engine and in order to be in time for school, he used to rise at 4.00 a.m. and get his work done first. Such men lived out the "Heart, Soul and Strength" maxim of Jesus and gave materially and spiritually all they possibly could of all they had, to maintain this Church at Colley Gate.

Slowly but surely the congregation grew, and in 1868 a small room was built by Mr. J. P. Bloomer for the Sunday School. It cost about £100 and was behind and slightly away from the chapel. Over 100 children could meet there in what was now a separate organisation. As for their seating, this was provided by planks that were supported by a few bricks at each end. This Sunday School had its own set of rules that were read out to the pupils by the secretary once a quarter, and it celebrated its Anniversary Day. At the one held in 1869, "a boy of 13 years of age was the preacher. His name was Master S. Walker, of Drews Cottages, Halesowen."

About seven years later, Samuel Jones founded a Young Men's Bible Class, which he was to lead for forty years. Soon after, young ladies were allowed to join at a fixed age and the group developed into Adult Bible Class. Samuel was a major figure in the life of Providence and in 1876 he was appointed secretary of a new Trust. The remaining seven trustees of the original body had realised that they needed more help. Numbers were rising in the Sunday School and more space was needed, but they were burdened still by the mortgage taken out in 1857. Accordingly fellow church members and workers were invited to become involved and the new Trust of eighteen members eventually took over the running of Providence. James Tate was their treasurer. One of the first things that he had to account for was the covering in of the space between the chapel and schoolroom. Pews were also added in the church and a gallery was built to increase seating.

The Sunday School rapidly became a vital facility for the youngsters of Colley Gate, but it was apparent that the building was no longer big enough to cater for all those who wanted to attend. James Tate and Samuel Jones were the only two active trustees left and were unable to help. Their fellows had died, emigrated or resigned. Consequently "an enthusiastic band of young men teachers was becoming impatient

The Young Men's Class in 1938.

and they decided to take matters into their own hands, as far as extensions were concerned". One day in 1886 they met and knocked down the old School in eight hours. Impressed by their keenness, many villagers joined them to put up a bigger and better new structure. They dressed all the bricks, prepared the foundations for the new buildings, and made everything ready for the contractors, Joseph M. Tate and Samuel Newby, who charged £350. The old Sunday School, as it now is, remains in use as a carpenter's shop by Alan Worton, Home Improvements.

Just under 40 years later another Sunday School was planned and on 8 July 1925 Mr Felix Fellows and Mr Caleb Parker (a former scholar) laid the memorial stones. Worshippers of all ages thrust themselves into fund-raising for the new place, and a box was kept by each Sunday School class and was opened every month. At last the job was done and on Thursday 10 December 1925 the building "was opened with a gold key by Mrs. Caleb Cox, the wife of a former Sunday School Superintendent and daughter of James Tate, one of the early pioneers and a member of the second Trust formed in 1876. It cost £3,592. Mrs Tate, the wife of the builder Joseph M. Tate, gave 400 chairs, and the Women's Weekday Class paid £125 for a grand piano from the Alhambra Theatre in Stourbridge, at a cost of £125. That money was pulled in by weekly gifts of 3d from each member and by the proceeds from concerts, bazaars, sausage suppers, and private gifts.

Folk responsible for raising funds 1960s. Derek Trickett is in the centre on the back and on his left is David Tate, the builder. His father, J. M. Tate, built the 1886 church and his grandfather was one of the founders of the 1856 church.

The congregation soon felt that the old chapel had served its purpose and so by 1927 it was decided to abandon it and move all services and meetings to the new building, thus bringing together the Sunday School and Church. Eventually it was decided that a purpose-built chapel was once again needed and in 1961 the Trustees bought six old houses and the land used by Mr Wilf Homer as a mini smallholding and upon which he kept pigs and chickens and grew vegetables. Two years later the present Providence Methodist Church was opened. Within it was incorporated the name stone "Providence" from the 1856 building. The builders were again Joseph M. Tate, but this time under the direction of his son, David E. Tate. There were other personal connections between the two buildings and church members who worked on both: Joseph Knowles was a bricklayer in 1925 and foreman in 1963; whilst Joseph Trickett was a bricklayer in both years. Church members Caleb Worton, a plasterer, and Dereke Trickett joined them on the new project.

By now an act of Parliament had discharged Methodist Trustees from their legal responsibilities and a new body of managing trustees oversaw the running of

Stone Laying in 1961. Fourth from right is Sir Alfred Owen and fourth from left is Walter Hodgetts, Mayor of Halesowen.

Providence. This group consists of members elected onto the Church Council. Quite rightly today's worshippers acknowledge the work of the early trustees. Some of them "never saw the fruition of their vision, but their vision gave us what we have today. It is right to remember their foresight, sacrifice and generosity on this the 150th year of Methodism in Colley Gate." Founded by those who devoutly believed in the providence of God, Providence Church still flourishes, still serves the community, and still has two Sunday services along with a Junior Church. The banner of Methodism now rests with the young. They cannot fail if they but follow the honest and faithful example of their forebears.

If you would like to know more about Providence Methodist Church in Colley Gate, Cradley please visit www.providence-methodist.org.uk.

Chapter 9

THE HAMSTEAD DISASTER

For all the hundreds of people gathered about the winding gear at Hamstead Colliery that March day in 1908, it was a grim and desolate scene. Silently they stood, all that great assembly of men, women and children, and gaunt-faced was each and everyone of them. Fear was scarred into their expressions, worry haunted their eyes and foreboding filled their senses. Fingers were pushed firmly into brows lined with deep furrows of concern, palms were rubbed anxiously upon thighs taut with pessimism and eyes were fixed intently upon the pithead. It was as if through the force of their collective thoughts and gaze that the watching folk could bring up from the depths of the earth their men who were entombed.

This was the day that was dreaded by any mining community, the day when the word disaster was forced from the throats of people who now feared the sound of their own voice. How the disaster had happened few knew, but all knew too well what it threatened. At about 5 o'clock in the morning on 4 March a fire had broken out 600 yards below ground, at the inset near the bottom of the downcast shaft. It was later thought to have been caused by some candles that were stored in a wooden box. The fire rapidly took hold and swept through the mine. It burned down wooden pit props, causing roofs to cave in, and sent wraith-like poisonous fumes down passageways so as to strangle the air.

Over 30 men were below ground and quickly a few were brought back safely to the surface, but so swiftly did the inferno overcome the mine that the others had little chance to escape. Desperately they tried to flee along narrow and low routes, striving with might and main to beat both rock falls and choking smoke. It must have been a living nightmare. The lights had all gone, bar for the frightening flames that leaped upwards and outwards and which sought out everything that they could destroy. Bloodied from cuts, choked by the lack of fresh air and blackened by the coal which they hewed at such a cost, just three more colliers made it to the lifting gear and were pulled to safety. With the sight of death in his eyes, the last to do so was F. Jones. Behind him were 25 men trapped far beneath the ground.

Once the extent of the disaster was realised, the call for help went out. It did not go unheeded. Like fishermen, miners were bonded in a brotherhood and were ever swift to seek to save their brothers who were in danger. Two mine rescue teams were dispatched to Hamstead. The one was from Tankersley Mine in Barnsley and the other was from Altofts Mine in Normanton, also in Yorkshire. Both brigades were experimental and were hoping that through their skills and special breathing apparatus they could save colliers in a smoke-filled pit. Indeed, the rescue attempt was one of the first to use self-contained breathing apparatus sets.

The Altofts Mine itself had been the scene of a disaster in 1887. A terrible explosion had devastated one seam at around three o'clock on a Saturday afternoon in October. The regular day-shift of workmen had left the pit two hours before, and as reported by Frank N. Wardell. Her Majesty's Inspector of Mines, "this was a matter of thankfulness, inasmuch as had the explosion taken place previous to this hour, there would probably have been about 400 persons in the mine". As it was 28 men were down the pit. Of these twenty were killed and eight injured, two of whom died from the effects of their injuries.

Knowing the pain of anguish themselves, the Yorkshire teams were at Hamstead within hours of the disaster – and whilst other men from Hamstead constructed air passages they covered

F. Jones, the last man to escape from the mine.

their faces with what looked like gas masks and descended below. The rescuers were fully aware of the peril into which they went. And still they went in. Led by Sergeant A. T. Wimbourne, the Tankersley chaps took with them a bird in a cage to help warn them if the air became too asphyxiating. Their first thought was for their fellow colliers and in their valiant attempts at deliverance they lost one of their own. He was John Welsby, who died on Friday 5 March. John had not been well and yet he went repeatedly into the heat of the mine. His determination and dedication led to his death, caused from heat stroke and probably by problems with his breathing apparatus. Rightly, John Welsby was acclaimed as a hero and was posthumously awarded the Edward VII Medal. Fittingly he is recalled in a Welsby Avenue in modern Hamstead.

Unhappily the rescue attempts were hindered by the coming together of unfortunate circumstances. The mine manager had only been in charge for some six weeks and had not had time to get to know either his men or the details of the mine.

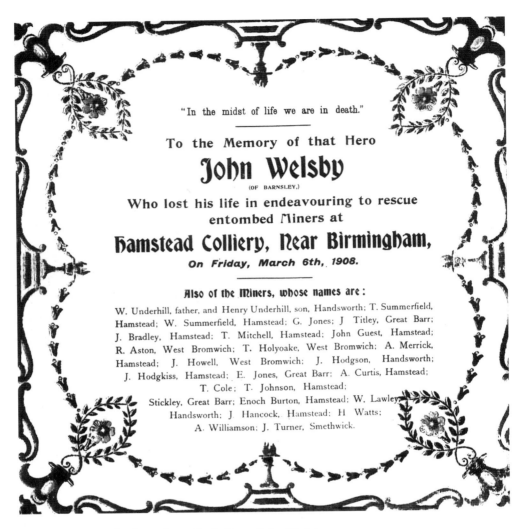

"In the midst of life we are in death."

To the Memory of that Hero

John Welsby

(OF BARNSLEY,)

Who lost his life in endeavouring to rescue
entombed Miners at

Hamstead Colliery, Near Birmingham,

On Friday, March 6th, 1908.

Also of the Miners, whose names are:

W. Underhill, father, and Henry Underhill, son, Handsworth; T. Summerfield,
Hamstead; W. Summerfield, Hamstead; G. Jones; J Titley, Great Barr;
J. Bradley, Hamstead; T. Mitchell, Hamstead; John Guest, Hamstead;
R. Aston, West Bromwich; T. Holyoake, West Bromwich; A. Merrick,
Hamstead; J. Howell, West Bromwich; J. Hodgson, Handsworth;
J. Hodgkiss, Hamstead; E. Jones, Great Barr; A. Curtis, Hamstead;
T. Cole; T. Johnson, Hamstead;
Stickley, Great Barr; Enoch Burton, Hamstead; W. Lawley,
Handsworth; J. Hancock, Hamstead; H Watts;
A. Williamson; J. Turner, Smethwick.

A memorial to the hero from Yorkshire, John Welsby.

His lack of knowledge was made worse by the sad fact that five days previously the under manager had been killed in a pit accident. Moreover, the main winding engines on the downcast shaft, where all the coal was drawn, had broken down two days before. Consequently coal drawing was suspended and so the man usually in charge of the downcast cage had been transferred to the upcast. Finally because of the heat in the upcast shaft caused by the furnace, the signal wires from the shaft bottom went up the downcast shaft. These were destroyed almost at the outbreak of the fire, leaving no proper means of signalling in the upcast.

The writer H. M. Tomlinson went to Hamstead at the time of the disaster and wrote an article called 'Pit Mouth'. He approached "the village of calamity with some awe and diffidence. You felt you were intruding; that you were a mere gross interloper, coming through curiosity, that was not excused by the compunction you felt, to see the appearance of a place that had tragedy in nearly all its homes. Young men streamed by on bicycles in the same direction, groups were hurrying there on foot."

As he went through the press of people to the colliery gates, "the women in shawls turned to me, first with annoyance that their watching should be disturbed, and then with some dull interest. My assured claim to admittance probably made them think I was the bearer of new help outside their little knowledge; and they willingly made room for me to pass. I felt exactly like the interfering fraud I was. What would I not have given then to be made, for a brief hour, a nameless miracle-worker."

Tomlinson was surprised that there was nothing to show "that somewhere half a mile beneath our feet were thirty men, their only exit to the outer world barred by a subterranean fire. Nothing showed of the fire but a whitish smoke from a ventilating shaft; and a stranger would not know what that signified. But the women did. Wet with the rain showers, they had been standing watching that smoke all night, and were watching it still, for its unceasing pour to diminish. Constant and unrelenting, it streamed steadily upward, as though it drew its volume from central fires that would never cease."

The writer watched as three Yorkshire rescue experts came out of the office. One of them was John Welsby. They had "muzzles on their mouths and noses, goggles on their eyes, fantastic helms, and queer cylinders and bags slung about them. As they went up the slope of wet ash, quick and full of purpose, their comical gear and coarse dress became suddenly transfigured; and the silent crowd cheered emotionally that little party of forlorn hope."

A postcard showing most of the men who died in the Hamstead Colliery Disaster, 4 March 1908. It also has shots of the colliery itself, the construction of an air passage, and of John Welsby, the rescuer who died attempting to save his fellow miners. John had come down from Barnsley with the Tankersely Brigade. Two of his pals are holding their breathing equipment, whilst W. Clifford on the left is carrying the canary which they took with them underground. Mrs Joan Jefferies told me several years back that "my mother, Florence and her sister Jinny, who were two of the Davies family daughters, used to tell me that it was their canary that was taken down the pit to warn if the air became too asphyxiating". Joan's gran and grandad lived at the Post Office in Hamstead.

Crowds gathered at the pit head at Hamstead Colliery, the scene of the Hamstead Disaster of March 1908.

Slowly the day passed at that "place from which came nothing but disappointment. Occasionally a child, too young to know it was adding to its mother's grief, would wail querulously. There came a time when I and all there knew that to go down that shaft was to meet with death. The increasing exhaustion and pouring sweat of the returning rescue parties showed that. Yet the miners who were not selected to go down were angry; they violently abused the favouritism of the officials who would not let all risk their lives."

Tragically, the entombed miners were not saved. It took a week following the fire for the mine to clear of the deadly fumes. Then on 11 March, the first three bodies were found. They were Abnor Williamson, aged 44 and a pikeman, who was lying on his back with his arms and legs outstretched; Ernest Jones, 31, a loader, who was lying on his face behind some tubs; and Joseph Titley, 25, another loader, who was lying face down in the middle of the road.

Soon after a second group of eleven dead men was found together, lying with their faces towards the floor and arms under their mouths. They were Richard Aston, 33, a haulage man; Enoch Burton, 39, a loader; Joseph Howell, 35, a deputy; Samuel Mitchell, 44, a stallman; Samuel Turner, 40, a loader; John Albert Hodgson, 29, a minder of dams; William Lawley, 27, another minder of dams; Walter Summerfield, 21, a haulage man; Charles Summerfield, 34, a stallman; and a father and son. They were William Underhill, 48, a stallman and Henry Underhill, 17, a driver. Both are buried at St. John's Church, Perry Barr. It is heartwrenching just to imagine the anguish of the wife and mother of this tragic family.

The next day six more bodies were recovered. They were found next to a board on which they had chalked their final message: "The Lord Preserve Us for We are All Trusting in Christ". In their death this valiant group left a message of courage, hope, dignity and, above all, of faith. They were Alfred (Arthur) Thomas Curtis, 34, a loader; John Guest, 27, a deputy; Henry Watts, 47, a loader; Thomas Cole, 34, another loader; Edward T. Johnson, 30, also a loader; and Joseph Hodgkiss, 17, a timekeeper, whose father had been killed a few years before at Hamstead. As they sat in the depths of the earth awaiting rescue – or more likely death, as they understood too well – they

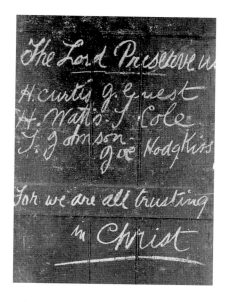

The last message of some the miners who died.

clung fast to their beliefs. Stoically and yet poignantly they scrawled their names and their belief and in doing so made plain their courage.

Finally on the afternoon of 14 March the last five men were found. They were James Bradley, 45, a haulage man; James Hancox, a driver of age unknown; Thomas Hollyoak, 39, a haulage man; Arthur Merrick, 23, a driver; and John Summerfield, 26, another driver. Of all the deceased whose addresses were known, two each came from Smethwick and Great Barr, three hailed from West Bromwich, and four lived in Handsworth. Eleven belonged to Hamstead itself. Just a small colliery village close to the Walsall Road, Hamstead was devastated by the loss of so many of its menfolk. Touched by the tragedy, the people of Brum and West Bromwich raised thousands of pounds for a relief fund to help the widows and their families.

Tomlinson was deeply affected by the disaster, "finding a new regard for my fellows since Great Barr. About you and me there are men like that. There is nothing to distinguish them. They show no signs of greatness. They have common talk. They have coarse ways. They walk with an ugly lurch. Their eyes are not eager. They are not polite. Their clothes are dirty. They live in cheap houses on cheap food. They call you 'sir'. They are the great unwashed, the mutable many, the common people. The common people! Greatness is as common as that. There are not enough honours and decorations to go round. Talk of the soldier! Vale (farewell) to Welsby of Normanton! He was a common miner. He is dead. His fellows were in danger, their wives were white-faced and their children were crying, and he buckled on his harness and went to the assault with no more thought for self than great men have in a great cause; and he is dead. I saw him go to his death. I wish I could tell you of Welsby of Normanton."

Today the pit has gone and Hamstead is another suburb within the West Midlands conurbation. But let us not cast from our minds the miners who dug the coal which powered us to industrial supremacy and let us pass on to our children's children the bravery of those colliers who died at Hamstead. They trusted in Christ. May they rest in His peace.

The Hamstead Colliery

Hamstead Colliery was opened following the successful mining of coal at the nearby Sandwell Park Colliery. Both mines were on the edge of the South Staffordshire Coalfield and had to be sunk to a great depth to reach the coal – as opposed to the worked out mines in the heart of the Black Country where the coal had been closer to the surface and easier to get at. The Hamstead Colliery Company was formed in April 1875, leasing 500 acres from G.C. Calthorpe of Perry Hall. Because of unexpected geological problems and water ingress, the first coal was not extracted until after 1878. At a depth of 1836 feet it was then the deepest coal mine in the world.

The coal was of a very good quality but it was difficult to extract and from the beginning the mine was plagued by periodic outbreaks of fire. On 11 November 1898 a bad fire broke out, signalled by dense smoke. There were 480 men at work in the mine. A bell was rung to warn of danger. Thankfully all were brought out in 24 minutes except for those men with the horses. There were 70 horses and all but two were saved. Isaac Meacham, the mine manager then went down the shaft with 80 men to fight this fire. It was to no avail. That night the men shovelled 150 cart loads of rubbish by the light of their Davy into the mouth of the pit and down the down-cast shaft. By the morning the up-cast shaft had been filled in. The fire took nearly twelve months to burn itself out.

Although no lives were lost the pit closure caused hardship for 300 mining families. Soup kitchens were opened in Hamstead and West Bromwich to help women and children and a fund was started to which all Black Country miners contributed. Agents from collieries elsewhere came to Hamstead to offer miners work in Wales and Yorkshire, amongst other places.

During the 1930s improvements were made both in the mine and in facilities for the miners, with a recreation ground, pit head baths and a new miners' institute. Sixty new houses were also built by 1938, which were let to employees at nominal rent. Following nationalisation in 1947, Hamstead came under the National Coal Board. Then in 1963 a large number of Durham miners came to work in Hamstead,

Colliers at Hamstead about 1900.

following the closure of pits in their county. They and their families lived in the new 'Durham Estate' off West Road. Unhappily just two years later British Coal stated that the mine was "no longer viable" and closed Hamstead. Three years beforehand the Coal Board had invested heavily in a mechanical digger that proved to be a costly mistake. It was only capable of removing a straight line of strata and the coal brought to the surface was thus heavily contaminated with rock which was the main reason for the lower profits. There is still an estimated 4.5 million tonnes of coal presently valued at 80 million pounds waiting to be mined at Hamstead.

After the closure of the pit, Hamstead Village gradually lost its coal mining traditions and sense of being a distinct mining community as it was absorbed into the West Midlands conurbation. It is the aim of the Hamstead Miners Memorial Trust not only to commemorate the men who died in the disaster of 1908 but also to honour all the miners who worked at the pit and to bring to the fore their lives and those of their families.

The Hamstead Miners Memorial Trust

During the middle of 2002 Ken Styler, a local Hamstead resident, organised a public meeting to discuss his vision for a lasting memorial to the Hamstead Miners. This was well attended by members of the local community and a Steering Group was elected to take the vision forward. Importantly it was felt that the memory of Hamstead's mining village, together with the miners who died in the 1908 disaster, was not given the respect and recognition it deserved and that local young people especially were not aware of the tragic event that happened in their community.

The steering group meets on a regular basis to take the project forward and during 2003 became a charity, changing its name from the Hamstead Miners Memorial Fund to the Hamstead Miners Memorial Trust. The committee members are: Ken Styler (chairman), Tony Ward (treasurer), Val Ward (secretary), Maureen Dacey, Tony Fowler, Reg Hackett and Brenda Styler. A founder member was Mrs. Brenda Harrison J.P., who was very active, particularly with fund raising. Brenda passed away in January 2005. At last the vision of the Trust was realised on Friday 13 June 2008 when thee was a grand unveiling of the monument in memory of the miners who worked and died in Hamstead Colliery. It is sited on at the corner of Hamstead Road and the Old Walsall Road. You can find out more about the Hamstead Mine and the Trust's superb website, www.hamsteadminers.co.uk

Chapter 10

BLOXWICH SPIRITUALIST CHURCH

Many years back I came across a rivetting autobiography. It was called *The Memoirs of a Maverick* and was by a Maurice Wiggin. Published in 1968 it was unusual as the chapters on the author's early life were set in Bloxwich, a place which I had never come across before in a published life story. Maurice later went on to write for national newspapers in London, but for me his importance lay in the fact that he was a keen and perceptive observer of Black Country life during the inter-war years. Proudly he asserted that "I am a child of the Black Country at its most attenuated and peripheral, the Black Country petering out into the green countryside of Cannock Chase; and also a child of the Industrial Revolution, which, when I was an infant living literally in the factory, was still in flow, saved from petering out, revivified and re-licensed, by the Great War of 1914-1918, which broke out when I was scarcely two".

Maurice's grandfather, James Thomas Wiggin, had been a man of standing locally. He began by forging horse furniture – bits, stirrups and bridle parts – for the leather trade in nearby Walsall. This lorinery he carried on in the brewhouse in the backyard. He was remembered as "as a great man in a small way". Tall, erect, trimly bearded and with piercing pale eyes he had a manner that "somehow combined autocracy with the benign aloofness of the contemplative man". A notable preacher who was much respected for actually practising what he preached, James Thomas was a practical man and with one of his sons, James Enoch, he founded the firm of J. and J. Wiggin. This grew into a major employer that gave work to hundreds of men and women locally.

Wiggin senior bought land and built workshops in Revival Street "and as a crowning stroke, wonderfully symbolical, he took over the Old Hallelujah Mission Hall". This old hall gave its name to a range of products that become well known nationally. After the First World War and under the leadership of uncles and cousins of Maurice Wiggin, the business diversified successfully into the manufacture of a wide range of chromium-plated bathroom accessories. Then in 1928 the adventurous decision was taken to make these and other products with a new stainless steel that did not rust and which contained 12% chromium, Appropriately called 'Staybrite', it was also used pioneeringly for the Old Hall stainless steel tableware, and in 1930 the company made the world's first stainless steel teapot in

Bloxwich. (For more on Old Hall see the Old Hall Club website of Nigel Wiggin at www.oldhallclub.co.uk).

Maurice's father, Samuel, was not involved in the business of J. and J. Wiggin. Instead he and his brother, Joe, had bought the firm of V. J. Broadhurst and Co on the road to Walsall. Both "could do anything they asked their workers to do, and they took the same risks". One of Maurice's earliest dramatic memories was "of seeing my father supported from the factory by two men, tottering, blood spurting from a gash around his eye. A flying splinter of white-hot metal gads had caught him." After lying unconscious on a sofa, Sam Wiggin recovered and with stitches in his cut went about his business. As his son observed, "colliers and iron workers need to be stoical. A man was lucky to come through his working life without being crippled. Little bumps and knocks were of no account; indeed they were valued as badges of manhood."

Later a builder and owner of a small farm on the Lichfield Road, Sam Wiggin eventually went back to work at Broadhurst's. He was a character in a world filled with quirky yet captivating folk. The son of a preacher in a Methodist stronghold, he "was frequently converted by visiting missionaries in the Old Hall". It came "natural to him to leap up from the bench and accept Jesus before the cocoa came round", and he was "utterly sincere". Originally Sam Wiggin was a staunch Wesleyan Methodist, belonging to a sect that was strong amongst small-scale factory owners and shopkeepers. His son and two daughters were sent to chapel for Sunday services both on the morning and the evening, with Sunday School sandwiched in between on the afternoon. But then about 1918 "Spiritualism was grafted on to this quite strong and fervent religiosity". This was a momentous shift, "the most climacteric move of our lives" and though "the connections with the rest of the family were warmly maintained, we were on our own from now on. And we charted a singular course."

Spiritualism as an organised movement had come to Britain from America in the 1850s, and by 1901 a National Spiritualists Union had been founded. It was based on seven principles: the Fatherhood of God; the brotherhood of man; the communion of spirits and the ministry of angels; the continuous existence of the human soul; personal responsibility; compensation and retribution hereafter for all the good and evil deeds done on earth; and eternal progress open to every human soul.

Although Spiritualism attracted well-known figures such as the writer Sir Arthur Conan Doyle and the scientist Sir Oliver lodge, its strength lay in working-class areas of England. Maurice Wiggin thought that his parents had learned about Spiritualism from Walsall, where there was a well-established church but he recalled that the Bloxwich National Spiritualist Society was actually founded by his uncle Ben, the brother of his mother. This unfortunate man had been in a serious accident down the pit when his back had been broken by a fall of coal. Come rain come shine, he was

The open air service at the opening of the Bloxwich Spiritualist Church in 1938. All the photographs in this chapter have been sent to me by Andy Browne from the collection of his mom, Mary Browne nee Daniels. As a small girl she watched the laying of the foundation stones of Bloxwich Spiritualist Church and still attends. I am most grateful to Andy and Mary for allowing me access to these rare photos. The emergence and growth of Spiritualism has been badly neglected by historians and it is only because I received these photos that it stirred in me a vague recollection that I had read something on spiritualism in Bloxwich a good few years back. That led me to scour my library until I came across the book by Maurice Wiggin. In itself this autobiography provides a singular insight into the development of spiritualism in the 1920s.

marked out by his "greenish bowler, a hard high come-to-Jesus collar, button boots, several layers of mustard coloured cardigan, a black jacket and pin-striped trousers, a greasy mac, and two or three scarves". Praised in the literature of the local Society as the founder and a vice president, Ben was manoeuvred out of the leadership of the local spiritualists by his brother in law. Sam Wiggin, as his son brought to mind, "simply loved organising and administering – did it very well, too".

The early meetings of the Spiritualists in Bloxwich were held "in a large cheerless rented room over the Co-op", in itself "a quite splendid building". But this meeting place "would never do for a family so root-conscious; we wanted the adventure all sewn up in a place that we could really call our own; and in 1920 or thereabouts we took over The Orl." This Spiritualists' Hall had previously been a garage and fruiterer's. The Wiggins and others threw themselves into transforming "a pretty dire building" into a suitable place of worship. Downstairs was social territory, where meetings were held and which had facilities for the making of tea and sandwiches and such like; but upstairs was the main worship room – the Temple of Light. Thus the Spiritualists' Hall fulfilled an important role, not only for those who worshipped there but also for those who came to socials with games and songs, fish and chip suppers, healing circles, séances and other events.

There was also a Sunday School called the Lyceum, but as Maurice stressed "when all's said and done, and glorious though the social contribution of the Orl was on weekdays, it was the big Sunday services, particularly the evening service, which put it apart from every other competing attraction. There was nothing quite like it." The Wiggins and their fellows may have been amateurs in religion but as such Maurice was certain that they were "a good deal more enthusiastic than the pros". This enthusiasm was coupled with the Black Country tradition that salvation was "something profoundly personal and man-to-man, like fighting; that religion was far too serious a business to be left to parsons". Such an egalitarian approach encouraged the emergence of powerful lay preachers. As Maurice declared, "a man might be poor, propertyless and unlettered, but if he had the gift of the gab, if he had the spark in him to get up and exhort us, why, we recognised it as a gift and gave him a respectful, or at least a polite, hearing".

Spiritualism in those days covered a wide range of beliefs, ranging from the "more scientific and almost secular" to the "more mystical and devout". However, in Bloxwich, according to Maurice, "our own variant was definitely a religion first" and "we called ourselves Christian Spiritualists, at any rate for a time". Hymns were sung from a spiritualist hymnal and meetings began and ended with a prayer, which was the "prerogative of anyone who happened to procure an invitation to sit on the chairman's right hand". Mostly Samuel Wiggin took the chair. Boasting "quite a presence" and a good voice, he arranged the seating on the platform. Around him were gathered the secretary, the speaker, the clairvoyant (sometimes the same person as the speaker), and the prayer maker; but "the whole set up was elastic and the chairman could invite just anyone he fancied to take a seat on the platform whether active in the meeting, or nor. It conferred status."

A day out from the church. Andy's aunt Martha is the right of the woman in black.

Maurice came from a family that had long been radical in its religion and their adherence to Spiritualism emphasised the distinctiveness and independence of the Wiggins. The prayer, whoever gave it, often "contained theological innovations of considerable daring. These passed unremarked; after all, we were innovators, rebels, reformers and radicals. Everyone looked at us askance, so we might as well give them something to look askance at." After the prayer came the address and a collection, which mostly consisted of coppers given the lack of wealth of most of the congregation, during which the

The church in the winter of 1941.

secretary read out the finances and a list of forthcoming events. Then there was a hymn, followed by the very reason of being for a Spiritualist church – the clairvoyance via a medium. Through the giving of messages from those who had departed to members of the congregation who could take a particular message, the clairvoyance provided "the thrilling extra which the other churches and chapels didn't have".

The Hall was a central fact in the life of the Wiggin family throughout the 1920s and Samuel "held some sort of honourific appointment in the wider Midlands area; the net was cast wide. We were always on the trot to far-flung Spiritualist churches and mediums from far afield were always coming to stay with us." Spiritualism was the faith around which the whole life of the family was centred: "we ate it and drank it, breathed it and slept it". Maurice himself moved away from Spiritualism but his parents remained staunch believers and their daughters followed them closely.

In common with the experience of so many new sects in the past, the Bloxwich Spiritualists were regarded with some suspicion in the Twenties but within a few years they had become more accepted. This change in attitudes was made plain by the election of Sam Wiggin as a councillor for the Birchills Ward on Walsall Town Council, where he became a chairman of the Housing Committee and a vice chairman of the Education Committee. The shift in views towards respectability was also marked by the building of "a fine new church, with an organ". After years of planning, the members had their own place of worship in the aptly-named Revival Street. It cost £700, about half the money was raised by "special efforts" whilst the rest came from loans from friends. Called the 'Temple of Light', the church was opened and dedicated to the Glory of God on 17 December 1938 with a large attendance. The principal stone was laid by Mr Samuel Wiggin, who had been president of the church since 1921 and who had also been a vice president of the National Spiritualist Church.

Over 40 stones were laid by various people, including one by Mr W. E. Washbourne of Wolverley in memory of his mother and father "who were the pioneers of spiritualism in Walsall". Another was laid by Mr John Tibbetts. Aged 87 he was regarded as "the father of spiritualism in the district"; whilst Mrs Haycock laid a stone in memory of her husband, Ben, who was the uncle of Maurice and was hailed as "the founder of Spiritualism in Bloxwich". The next day the first service was held. Mr Wiggin was

Lucy and Samuel Wiggins with a group outside the new church. The man with the beard on the left is John Tibbetts. Aged 87 he was regarded as "the father of spiritualism" in Bloxwich.

the speaker and Mrs Blewe the clairvoyant. Then in June 1939 a trip was arranged for church members to the Wolverley estate of Mr Washbourne, who kindly provided tea. It was a beautiful day and presents for races and games were paid for out of funds

The Temple of Light decorated for Easter. Sam Wiggin is on the far right and Andy's aunt, Mary Ann, is on the far left.

raised by the spiritualists themselves. On returning to Bloxwich, Mrs Vale gave everyone a commemorative handkerchief.

The Wiggins continued to be active in their faith until their deaths. Lucy died in the summer of 1960 aged 79. Maurice wrote that she had been told by a medium that she would pass away suddenly, in the afternoon, with her family around her. One Saturday afternoon indeed "she was in the old family Rover, with my father driving and my elder sister on the back seat, on their way to have their Sunday ritual high tea with my younger sister and her little brood. Half-way between the two homes, which were only a mile or

The golden wedding anniversary of Lucy and Sam Wiggin in 1939. They are third and fourth from the left on the first seated row. I think that Maurice Wiggin is to the right of his mother.

two apart, she had a heart attack and died." Though someone who took joy in life, Lucy had approached the end "with an ever-deepening conviction that death was but a portal through which she had to pass to rejoin her loved ones who had gone before, and to await in glory the loved ones who would follow. She had total faith. She enjoyed her life to the very end and she enjoyed her certainty that the end was but a beginning." Her husband, Samuel, died soon after of a broken heart. Both have left a lasting legacy for Bloxwich National Spiritualist Union continues to thrive in Revival Street and like all such churches it relies on the goodwill and dedication of volunteers like the Wiggins.

Chapter 11

A BLACK COUNTRY HERO

The Kaiser thought his great army would sweep in to the sea that small force of British soldiers sent to help the French when war with Germany broke out on 4 August 1914. So sneering was he of the British Expeditionary Force that he commanded his forces to 'exterminate first the treacherous English and walk over General French's contemptible little army'. Massively outnumbered, yet the gallant British regulars were not overwhelmed. They proved to be tough and dogged opponents, who were skilled and swift marksmen with their Lee Enfields.

By early October, the British Expeditionary Force had already come to blows with a much greater German force at Mons and had been forced to retreat, despite superior riflemanship and battle craft; whilst the French had suffered a heavy defeat at Charleroi. That dismaying and demoralising retreat ended on 6 September when the French and British counter-attacked at the Battle of the Marne, which was followed swiftly by the bloody Battle of the Aisne.

Pushed back and held back by the Allies, the Germans had not abandoned hope of a quick victory that would be achieved by breaking through the Allied lines and capturing Calais and Boulogne – thus all but cutting off France from reinforcements from Britain. They launched a fierce attack that became the 1st Battle of Ypres – a town in Flanders that was recalled by many a British Tommy as Wipers. The battle raged between 18 October and 18 November. Its course has been aptly described as "extremely bitter and massively confused" by John Bourne, an expert on British involvement in the First World War.

The 1st Battalion South Staffordshire Regiment, part of the 22nd Infantry Brigade of the British 7th Division, was in the thick of that momentous battle in which the British Expeditionary Force suffered 50,000 casualties and the French many more. That vast and impersonal number hides 50,000 individuals who were wounded or killed, 50,000 individuals whose lives were wrecked, and 50,000 individuals each of whom had a horrible individual experience that was shared by others. Individuals like the brothers Jim and Tom Pumfrey who were both killed on 28 October whilst serving with the 1st Battalion the South Staffordshire Regiment. Hailing from Upton-on-Severn in Worcestershire, they have no known grave and are commemorated on the Menin Gate Memorial to the Missing, Ypres. And individuals like Captain J. S.S. Dunlop, whose bravery and death was brought to the fore by one of his men, Pte. John Jones.

Captain Dunlop led B Company into Polygon Wood to reinforce the Northumberland Hussars. As they advanced they approached a farm house in a clearing in which was a German machine gun. Captain Dunlop did not hesitate. Crying, "Come on, men!" he led his men in a charge. The house was taken but unfortunately Captain Dunlop was killed.

Private Jones was there at his officer's death. He later wrote movingly that:

One of the bravest was our Captain, and as good as a father to all his men. I shall always remember when he got killed. Having got through a wood alright, we started to advance across a ploughed field. We had no sooner got into the open than the Germans began shelling us, they had got the range. I had just dropped down when a shell burst behind me, and the force of the explosion hurled a pig about ten yards, the animal landing near me. Though surprised for a moment I found the carcass useful cover. Our Captain was a man who knew his work, and the men would go anywhere with him. The order was given for a bayonet charge, and we had not gone far across the ploughed field before the Captain was killed. When he was killed I think our fellows went mad. They gave the Germans something to go on with, the place swarmed with dead after the charge. When we got back to where the Captain lay some of our fellows had a job to keep tears from their eyes, they loved him so well.

Officers of the 1st Battalion South Staffordshire Regiment at Corbie, Bray-sur-Somme, May 1916. South Staffordshire Regiment photos taken from James P. Jones', A History of the South Staffordshire Regiment from 1705-1923.

Day after day, the British were assailed and day after day they repulsed the Germans. The battle's crisis came on 31 October when the enemy broke through the thin British line at Gheluvelt on the Menin Road and looked set to forge ahead to Ypres. The day was saved by a valiant charge of the 2nd Battalion Worcestershire Regiment. Gheluvelt was recaptured and the British lines was re-established.

Vicious fighting went on to overwhelm the early days of November. Major-General T. Capper, C.B., D.S.O. , who commanded the 7th Division, later wrote that "on November 7th the 1st Battalion South Staffordshire Regiment, although very weak after three weeks' fighting, made a gallant counter-attack in support of the First Corps, which was hard pressed, driving the enemy from his trenches and assisting in the capture of three machine guns. This effort at the end of three weeks' continual fighting - and with hardly any Officers left, speaks eloquently for the bearing of this Battalion."

It was in this attack that Captain J. F. Vallentin showed outstanding courage. Previously he had been wounded slightly and was in hospital at Ypres when on 6 November he heard that his Regiment was going into action that night. Determined to be with his comrades Captain Vallentin obtained permission to rejoin them. During the subsequent assault on the German trenches he was twice wounded. Unheeding of his injuries he pressed on until he was killed by five or six machine gun shots. The capture of the trenches owed much to the confidence held in his valiant leadership by his men. Captain J. F. Vallentin was awarded a posthumous Victoria Cross "for conspicuous bravery" This was the first V.C. won by the South Staffordshire Regiment in the war, and the first one ever awarded to the 1st Battalion, the old 38th.

By now the battered, gallant battalions of the British Expeditionary Force existed only in name, so terrible had been their losses in this battle of attrition from which they did not shrink. The South Staffs suffered as grievously as any. The 1st Battalion was pulled back from the Front just days before the end of the 1st Battle of Ypres. When it had landed in Belgium just a few weeks before it had been a force of 1,100 officers and men. Now only 78 remained. Almost every officer had either been killed or wounded, and only one N.C.O., Company Sergeant Major F. Bytheway, was left to bring the men out of action.

For most of that year the Battalion was in the trenches. The misery of trench warfare was broken up by the Battles of Neuve Chapelle (10-12 March),

Captain J. F. Vallentin, who was awarded the Victoria Cross posthumously.

Festubert (15-27 May) and Loos (25 September-8 October). All three were British assaults on the German lines that sought to divert German attention away from French attacks. All three were planned and prepared meticulously. And all three failed in their objectives. The outnumbered British troops made it clear that they could capture German positions, but it was impossible to hold them without greater manpower.

At Loos, the 1st Battalion South Staffs went into action at 6.28 a.m. on the first day. The order to "Get ready to charge" came down the line, and Lieutenant W. Cooper instructed the scouts and wire-cutters to advance. Straight afterwards, C Company climbed up the ladders and moved on through the dense smoke screen made by the British with smoke bombs, smoke candles and gas. The forbidding gloom was darkened even more by a thick cold mist and drizzling rain.

The Battalion War Diary recorded that:

> Lieut. W. Cooper led his men on with the utmost gallantry, and was killed on the German wire. He was a most gallant Officer, loved and respected by all ranks. 'A' Company came on splendidly, ably led by Captain Henry de Trafford, who behaved with the greatest coolness and daring. He fell on the German wire, and his last words were, 'Don't mind me; push ahead.' Truly he and Lieut. Cooper, and the other brave Officers, N.C.Os and men, who fell on this fateful day, deserve the undying gratitude of their country and their Regiment. Lieut. Bell, with 'A' Company, did excellent work, and proved himself – as at Festubert – a leader of men. 'D' Company, led by Captain O. Limbery, did gallant work under their young commander, who, with many others, was wounded. 'B' Company, under Lieut. H. J. Burke, was the Reserve Company in fourth line, and were very well led by this young Officer, who displayed much bravery and keenness. He was, unfortunately, killed during the advance.

After storming the first German line, the 1st Battalion took the second and support line, and mixed up with other regiments, it went on to capture a position called "The Quarries". Unhappily, they had to pull back in the face of a strong German counter attack. From 27 to 30 September, the 1st South Staffords "did magnificent work, under every description of fire. Fierce counter-attacks by the German bombers were repeatedly checked by our own bombers, who continually went to the assistance of the hardly pressed Regiments on their right and left flanks." Their colonel, Lieutenant Colonel R. M. Ovens, declared that "time after time the call 'Staffordshire bombers this way!' was heard, and never was that call for help left unanswered. The Germans made attack after attack down from 'The Quarries' towards their old front line, and were as often driven back by the magnificent steadiness and splendid counter-bombing of the old 38th (1st South Staffords). The endurance and steadfast British pluck of these brave men undoubtedly repeatedly saved the situation."

The Battalion went into the Battle of Loos with 21 officers and 729 N.C.Os and men. Of these, nine officers were killed, 8 eight were wounded, and one died later from his wounds; whilst 430 N.C.Os and men were killed or wounded. A few days later on 13 October, the South Staffs were prominent in the attack on the Hohenzolern Redoubt, a German stronghold. Tragically, amongst those who were killed were the brothers John and Richard Stephens, who were from Wimblebury near Cannock. Neither of them has a known grave and both are commemorated on the Loos Memorial to the Missing.

As important and as brave as the counter bombers in the Battle of Loos was the 1st Battalion's machine gun detachment. It was commanded by Lieutenant G. B. Schon, who "displayed such tenacity, bravery and skill during these six days that he was subsequently honoured by an 'Immediate' award of the Military Cross. The detachment did magnificent work under his direction." It is probable that David Appleby was one of this machine gun detachment which was so conspicuous in its courage for the 1st Battalion, and he later went on to become a corporal in the Machine Gun Corps.

David had joined the 4th South Staffordshires in 1912 as a sixteen-year old. The 4th was a special reserve battalion and was mobilised on 3 August 1914, the day before war was declared, after each man was contacted by a card. A few days later the battalion was sent to Jersey. His daughter, Sheila has her father's medals. They include the 1914 Star with the 'bar' on it and Sheila was told by the Staffordshire Regimental Museum that this indicated that he had served in France and/or Belgium under fire up to 22 November 1914 with the 1st Battalion South Staffords. This particular battalion was stationed in South Africa at the outbreak of war and returned to England on 19 September. Thence it left for Belgium on 4 October, where it was soon involved in action. David must

Brigadier General R. M. Ovens C.M.G., commander of the 1st Battalion South Staffordshire Regiment 1914-1916.

David Appleby and his wife in about 1920. Thanks to Sheila Appleby.

have joined the 1st Battalion as a reinforcement, either before it went or soon after it had arrived.

As for the Machine Gun Corps this was created by Royal Warrant on 14 October 1915, followed by an Army Order on 22 October. Before then the few machine guns available to the British were attached in sections to individual battalions. At the outbreak of war, two Maxim machine guns were allocated to each infantry battalion, although this was later increased to four. These were served by a subaltern and twelve other ranks. They had a maximum rate of fire of 500 rounds, the equivalent of about 40 well-trained riflemen.

With the formation of the Machine Gun Corps, the Maxims were withdrawn from the battalions and replaced by Lewis guns, many of which were made at the BSA in Small Heath, Birmingham. Soon after, the Maxims were taken out of service with the Machine Gun Corps in favour of Vickers machine guns. Fired from a tripod that weighed 20 pounds, the Vickers gun itself weighed 28½ pounds and was cooled by water held in a jacket against the barrel and which weighed another ten pounds. The maximum rate of fire was 500 rounds per minute, which lasted thirty seconds. Two men carried the equipment and two the ammunition, and there were two spare men to each machine gun detachment.

Most Machine Gun Companies took their number from the Infantry Brigade to which they were attached. David Appleby was in 6th Company and this meant he was attached to the 6th Brigade. He was one of an elite group. The men of the Machine Gun Corps had to be well built, fit and capable of working effectively in a small team. From the first it was insisted the men of the Machine Gun Corps had to be

David Appleby as a dashing young sergeant in the First World War. David was the father of Sheila Appleby who proudly wrote to me about her father's service in the First World War. Thanks to Sheila Appleby.

of the highest calibre. 6th Company was attached to the 2nd Division in January 1916 and as such took part in the Battle of the Somme. This began at 7.30 a.m. on 1 July 1916 and lasted 141 days. It took on the shape of a major campaign with separate battles within it. Lloyd George declaimed it as "one of the most gigantic, tenacious, grim, futile and bloody fights ever waged in the history of war".

Over several months, the British lost over 400,000 men. Whole units, such as the Accrington Pals, were all but wiped out, plunging the entire population of towns into mourning. No major enemy position was captured and there was no breakthrough – although Field Marshall Haig asserted that the battle had relieved pressure on the French at Verdun, drawn German reserves away from the fight with the Russians on the Eastern Front, and eroded the fighting capacities of the German Army. That was so, and it also demoralised the Germans – although that was not obvious at the time.

It seems that it was during the Battle of the Somme that David Appleby gained the honour of a Military Medal. This award was first instituted in March 1916 for distinguished service in the field for Warrant Officers, NCOs and lower ranks. All awards of the Military Medal were announced in the London Gazette with no citation. David's daughter, Sheila, has a copy of his announcement. It is dated 21 October 1916 and states that "His Majesty the King has been graciously pleased to approve the award of the Military Medal for bravery in the Field to the undermentioned Non-Commissioned Officers and Men: - Included in the list of awards is the name of:- 16074 Cpl D. Appleby 6th Coy., M. Gun Corps."

Normally the event for which the award was made had taken place between three and four months before, which would have placed David Appleby's courageous action in the early stages of the Battle of the Somme. His daughter, Sheila tells me that "the town's people of Willenhall made a presentation to David Appleby when he was awarded the Military Medal, a gift of a gold pocket watch. It was reported in the local paper but the article has long since vanished sadly."

Although David survived the war, he did not come through that terrible conflict unscathed. He was wounded and suffered in a gas attack. I have contacted Dr John Bourne to ask his advice about finding out what David did to gain his Military Medal. John informed me that "there are no surviving medal citations for the Military Medal in the Great War, so the only hope of finding out why Corporal Appleby was honoured is in the War Diary of 6th Brigade. There is a possibility of some mention of the act that won the medal but I would not bet on it. These War Diaries are in the National Archives: Public Record Office, Kew, in record series WO 95. The day of the award is not the day of the act, so it is difficult to work out from that what he might have been doing."

Whatever the case, David Appleby was a man of whom the Black Country should be proud. He was a brave soldier in an elite unit. Nicknamed the Suicide Club, the Machine Gun Corps played a vital role both in defence and attack and as such was targeted heavily by the enemy. There is a memorial to the Machine Gun Corps in Hyde Park. The inscription reads: "Saul has slain his thousands but David his tens of thousands." David Appleby was one of those Davids.

Chapter 12

TELLING IT AS IT WAS

Kathleen Hann was driven to set down her story by anger and pain and by a compelling need to write working-class history from within. Fiercely proud of her Black Country roots and of her working class identity, she never thought that she would record her experiences but that became her mission following her unhappy experience at a university open day that she attended with her daughters. Both were mature students and they took their Mom with them to a talk given by "a highly educated middle-class lady historian".

This academic spoke at great length about working-class women in the 1930s but there was no warmth in her delivery, nor any empathy with the folk whose lives had been burdened by hardships and poverty and who had struggled to get by as best they could. Instead "the woman seemed so very cold and clinical. She spoke of Mrs A and Mrs B, and of how twenty percent of women did one thing and thirty percent did another thing and so on."

Furious and at the same time hurt at the way the lives of her mother and grandmother had been reduced to statistics, Kathleen stood up to speak but her anger and pain got in the way of her speech. She stumbled and cried. Upset with herself as much as with the historian with whom she wished to remonstrate, Kathleen's Black Country accent became more pronounced as she struggled to fetch out her feelings. She wanted to state clearly that working-class history should be written by working-class people, that it was our past upon which the speaker was pronouncing so coldly and mater-of-factly. This woman may have had all the details right, but Kathleen wished that she herself "had the clearness of mind when standing up in the hall full of young women to tell that historian that history is about *more* than facts and figures – it's about people. *Real* people."

After what she thought were her stumbling attempts at speaking Kathleen sat down to deafening silence. She wanted the floor to open up and swallow her, but then to her amazement there was a loud noise. Kathleen turned around "to see all those students standing up and clapping. *It took some time to realise the applause was for me.*" The younger women came up to the older woman who had shocked them with her ardour and they shook her hand, asking and demanding that she should "tell it as it was".

Her passion about her people had welled up deep inside her and Kathleen knew she had to write it down as she saw it, that she had to bring to the fore the fact that history is about "pain, hurt, hunger, disappointment, humiliation, but most of all it's about the utter frustration of living (no, not living, *existing*) from one pay day to another – the never, never ending slog of the treadmill".

Impelled by her determination and fervour, Kathleen could do only one thing. She knew she could get all the facts and figures about, say, the Black Hole of Calcutta and write them all down but "I couldn't write about it with great feeling and depth because I wasn't there. But I can and I will write with feeling and compassion about the Black Country working-class people of the thirties – because that was where I spent my short childhood."

Kathleen aged 21. Photographs thanks to Kathleen Hann.

Fired by the urge to put pen to paper, Kathleen went straight home after the lecture and wrote throughout the night. Pages and pages were covered "but the most weird and frightening thing is that when I re-read what I had written it seemed like someone else had written down the information – for there were things there I didn't realise I knew about". With her sensations and her soul taking over, Kathleen had had pulled out of her sub-conscious mind information that had lain dormant for many years. Overwhelmed by the strangeness and the scariness of what had happened, she did not sleep. Then the next morning Kathleen rang her elder sister and asked her about the things that had been stirred up by the tumult of her emotions and "she confirmed everything I had written down".

Writing it down was not to be an easy thing. Kathleen had to confront distressing memories that she had pushed to the back of her mind and which she had thought she had left behind; she had to dust down long-hidden thoughts that raised up doubts, anguishes, aches and grievances. It was painful for her to remember "and many, many times my tears have smudged the pages when putting pen to paper and I have wiped my eyes and started again". Her mind scraged by her emotions, yet still she went on. She wrote as she felt. She wrote in her own style. She wrote because "this is me".

Most of all Kathleen wrote it for her mom and her kind, the selfless, doughty, ever-working mothers of the Black Country. As she stresses, her mother "was the very best teacher I ever had. She taught me survival, she taught me the family is the all-important; but most of all she taught me love and compassion. Like me she left school at the age of fourteen. She had very little schooling, but she had more commonsense in her little finger than lots of people have in their whole bodies."

This then is Kathleen's social history. She knows that it will never gain her a degree or even an O-Level, but that is not what is important to her now – even though once that would have been so important for her. It had always been an impossible and unheard-of dream for Kathleen to have gone to university, yet now that had fallen by the wayside compared to "the magic and beauty of the creative process". Her social history would explain and get through "to all those young girls about the hardships of life in the thirties" and it would do more, for through the making of it and the living of it Kathleen herself learned some very hard lessons that she could never have been taught at any university and "which the historian, for all her education, will never, never comprehend".

Born 1930 at the old fire station yard in High Bullen in the heart of Wednesbury, Kathleen was the seventh of eight children. Her poor mother had lost her first two babies when they were just a few days old and her next two both had pneumonia. There was no penicillin then and pneumonia killed. Kathleen's mom wrapped her babbies in cotton wool and nursed them for 21 days, through what was thought of as the crisis time. Thankfully both Eric and Jesse recovered thanks to the careful nursing, although another child was to die aged just eighteen months.

Home was a small, badly-built and totally inadequate back-to-back shared with Grandma. She slept in one bedroom, Kathleen and her four siblings in the other. The two lads shared one bed and the three wenches another. A rope was strung across the middle of the room and "Mom had draped old curtains and worn-out blankets across the line to give us some small privacy". The youngsters could talk through the curtains and the boys would tell jokes and stories, "but none of us were allowed to move the curtain or cross that line except to go in and out of the room". As for Kathleen's mother and father, they slept in the tiny living room downstairs, although how they did so remains a mystery for there seems to have been no bed or any comfort.

At the back of the houses was a brew house shared by four families. Each woman did her washing on a different day. The wash house had only a cold water tap and an old boiler that had to be stoked up every day – and in those days washing was hard collar and a full day and often much of the night was taken over by boiling, scrubbing, swilling and mangling the clothes. When all that backbreaking and arm aching work was done, the maiding tub would be tipped up and the soapy water would be emptied into the yard so that it could be swept down and made clean.

Unfortunately, there was only one toilet between the four families and Kathleen recoils from its unpleasant memories:

It was terrible if you were in a hurry to use it, especially if one of the men had been smoking dog ends (the bits of tobacco saved from used cigarettes and then re-rolled). The smell would be awful! Each person had to take their own pieces of paper with them. There were no luxuries like toilet paper in those days, and even if there had been we wouldn't have been able to afford any. I recall one boy being rushed to hospital because he had used paper from a magazine that still had a metal clip in it; the clip had wedged into his backside and he had to have an operation to remove it. The teasing he received from anyone by far outweighed the pain he suffered.

Life was an ongoing struggle for Kathleen's mom in particular, as it was for all moms. She cleaned, polished, scrubbed and tried to make a decrepit old house a place that was fit to bring up her children in. But it was a losing battle. There were fleas that woke up the youngsters and left big red-bite marks over them, and bugs in the brickwork that stank the place with a sweet, awful sickly smell. That vile stench will remain with Kathleen for ever. I was lucky that I never had to draw it in but Our Mom did. She came out of a back house in Whitehouse Street, Aston and in the early 1950s used to burn the bugs off the ceiling in the attic with a candle before she went to bed. Our Mom still shudders at the smell saying it was revolting and that it never left your nostrils even though mothers wore themselves out striving to keep their homes clean.

Kathleen and Peter at their wedding in 1951.

Kathleen's mom was of that ilk. She believed that cleanliness was next to godliness and it must have been sheer hell for her not to shift that reek – just as it must have been sheer hell for her to put up with the indignity of receiving hand outs. Unemployment ravaged England in the hungry thirties and many a proud man had his pride forced back into his craw because he could not keep his family. Kathleen's Dad was one of them. He was one of the millions who suffered. Fifty years old when his seventh child was born, he was ill with bronchitis and was mostly out of work. As such he had to go on to the Parish, as it was called.

These were the days of the hated Means Test when a man came round to the houses of the jobless and assessed their means. Anything of value had to be sold and folk had to live off that before they could claim a pittance to survive on. Kathleen understood only too well the ignorance of the officials:

Kathleen and Peter with their oldest child, Janet, in 1953.

People were only allowed the very bare essentials to live on. What the people from the parish didn't realise with all their great wisdom was that people had already sold any valuables they had ever possessed, and that only when they had reached rock bottom and hadn't enough money to feed their children would they finally go cap in hand to the parish.

A proud lady, Kathleen's mom was shamed by asking for 'charity' and her daughter was certain that "she would have starved rather than ask for help for herself, but she had to swallow her pride for the sake of her children. She had long sold the only thing of value she had, her wedding ring. In its place she wore a penny curtain ring from Woolworth's on her third finger left hand.

Kathleen is still angered by the thoughts of her mom's humiliation. I feel her anger. My Great Granny Wood was like Kathleen's mother, a strong woman, proud and caring. She laid out the dead of the street, she brought babbies into the world and she knew old remedies – and never did she charge for her help. It was given freely as a good neighbour. Then my great granddad was given his cards during the Depression. For as long as he could he wouldn't go on the Means Test because of the dishonour and when finally he had too because he couldn't find work and his kids were clammed he had a nervous breakdown. He felt degraded that someone could walk into his home without his say so and tell him what was what and how he should live. By then my great granny had also sold her wedding ring and was forced into the embarrassment of a brass curtain ring to save her shame.

The disgraces heaped upon the poor did not end there. They welled up into a relentless wave of mortification. Often the poor were not given money, instead they were grudgingly handed tokens. These could be exchanged only at certain shops. The memories of exchanging those tokens still haunt Kathleen for "the butcher would only supply offal, the baker would supply stale bread, and if we were lucky we would have a few stale cakes. The greengrocer would give bruised vegetables and occasionally bruised fruit." But Kathleen's family had no choice, they had to take whatever was given to them

Kathleen aged 74.

For all those dire days, there were moments of happiness, like when Kathleen's dad taught her arithmetic long before she started school. He also played dominoes with her, whilst he and his wife enjoyed crib. Kathleen kept the score for them, moving the spent matchsticks up and down the board.

One occasion with her father still remains strong with her. It was when she was just two or three and crowds gathered outside their house and her dad held her high on his shoulders "when the circus came to town, and I watched elephants parading along the High Bullen, Wednesbury".

A few years later, when Kathleen was still young, the great day came that her mother had longed for. The family had been allocated a new four bedroomed house. Kathleen holds fast the changes that move made and its wonderful effects on her mother, especially:

How happy she was! She went around in a dream. All the furniture was scrubbed and polished, to make sure it would be right for the new house. I believe the rent was eight shillings – a large amount and double the rent of the old house. My mom, though, was a great optimist and a very determined lady. She had made up her mind that her children were going to have a better home and we were going to have that house come what may. Although mom was a kind and generous woman where the health and happiness of her children were concerned, she could be a tigress. We never went hungry, though I'm quite sure that she did.

The poor working-class people were down and the system intended that they should stay down. They were meant to know their place and their place was at the bottom of the pile.

It was a constant struggle to pay the rent but pay it she did – and all her struggles were worth it for her and her chap to have their own bedroom and for her three wenches and two lads to be able to go to bed in separate rooms. Kathleen's mother went around the house in a dream. She loved every part of it "but her favourite place was the bathroom with its big white clean bath and lovely hot water straight out of the tap – a luxury she never had before". Each morning she would get up at six just to have a soak and "when we had a bath we all knew we had to leave the bath spotlessly clean, without any tidemarks or we would have been in real trouble". Mind you an old lady nearby was not as enchanted by the bath, for she made ginger beer and lemonade in it. Children went round with their own bottles to be filled up for a penny. The old girl would take the bottle and thrust her hand into the pop in the bath, "sometimes sticking her arm in right up to her elbow and scooping up the concoction".

But for Kathleen the bathroom had a very different purpose. She was a bookworm and the only one in the family to boot. Whenever she started to read in the crowded living room she was teased by her brothers and sisters. The rough and tumble of family life made it impossible for her to escape into her world of dreams, so she needed somewhere else to let her mind roam. Taking a cushion with her she found that place in the bathroom. It may not have had a chair but it had two distinct advantages: it was the only room in the house that boasted a lock, and the back boiler of the fire was located there, "which meant that apart from the living room it was really warm enough to linger in". By contrast the bedroom was freezing cold and shared with two sisters.

From the airing cupboard Kathleen would take two blankets, one of which would be placed longways in the bath. The cushion would be put at the opposite end to the taps, after which the dogged reader would take off her shoes, climb into the bath and wrap the other blanket around her. Kathleen was now able to embark on her great adventures and she felt that she was "the greatest escapologist since Houdini, living and breathing my wonderful world of books".

Little would that young Black Country wench have realised that one day she would not look in on that wonderful world of books but instead she would be part of it. Driven to write by a female historian who enraged her she may have been, but Kathleen could never have contemplated writing if it had not been for her love of words and her desire to tell not only her story but the story of her Mom and those others who touched her, encouraged her and inspired her.

Kathleen you have told your tale well. You have kept your people alive. You have made plain their adversities and sufferings but you have also brought out their humanity and their resilience. A people forced to the bottom of the pile by an unjust and arrogant system they may have been, but never were they cowed, broken in spirit, or made hopeless. They toiled and moiled hoping one day we would break free of the tyranny of class prejudice and that our kind would have choices in our lives. We still have not built that New Jerusalem and there remains much to do to bring about true equality, but our lives now are the better for the sacrifices they made. Thanks to you and writers like you, we shall never forget those who came before and to whom we owe so much. Keep on telling it as it was.

Kathleen Hann is the author of two books. The first inspired this article and is called *Telling It As It Was* (Writers' Club Press: 2002 ISBN 0-595-227900-2). It tells of Kathleen's early life and takes her story up to the time she was 21 and married her husband, Peter. The second is *Still Telling It As It Was* (Trafford Publishing: 2005 ISBN 1-4120-5535-0). This recounts her early married life in the Black Country from 1951 up to her move to Telford in 1969. With her husband Peter, just demobbed, they face financial hardship due to low wages and high housing costs. Bringing up three children at the time, Kathleen shows her love, care, mettle and great skills with "make do and mend" which have been passed on by her mother.

Each book is £10.99 (including free post to Great Britain for one or two books), or £20 for the two. They are available from Kathleen's son-in-law, David Harris, at 35, St Michael's Close, Telford, Shropshire, TF7 5SD, or via the world wide web. just Google for "kathleen hann still telling it as it was".

The kind of house in which Kathleen spent her earliest years; this one was in Trow's Square, off Wednesbury Road, in 1933. The photograph is taken from a cracking publication by Ian M. Bott, Wednesbury Memories (Sutton Publishing, £12.95). Ian has done a tremendous job in emphasising the history of Wednesbury and its people and he is one of a small but steadfast band of dedicated Black Country historians resolved to ensure that the past of various towns is brought forward into the present and the future. He has written a number of books on Wednesbury and like his previous publications, this one brings out of the shadows and into the glare of history a superb collection of photographs that bring life to the history of the town.

Chapter 13

PORTOBELLO:
THE BEAUTIFUL GATE

Say "Portobello" to most people and straight away they would think of the world-famous Portobello Market in London, made even more familiar and well known by the film 'Notting Hill'. Today this Latin-sounding name conjures up bustling crowds, appealing pubs, fruit and veg traders, sellers of second-hand goods, dealers in antiques, and vendors of fashionable clothes. It is a colourful, exciting scene that seems to fit well an exotic-sounding name – and yet the origins of Portobello owe nothing to peace and harmony, although they are inextricably tied into the buying and selling of goods.

From the sixteenth century when the Spanish conquered a huge empire in Central and South America, they were determined to ensure that only Spain would benefit from the wealth that they took from their territories. This restriction of trade increasingly led to clashes with the British, a people who saw themselves as a sea-faring folk who had the right to trade with whosoever they might please and wheresoever they might wish. Many British merchant ships secretly sought out opportunities to buy goods. The profits were high, but so were the risks – for if captured by the Spanish authorities the vessel and its cargo would be confiscated.

Other British seamen were more belligerent, becoming buccaneers who attacked and captured Spanish ships and sometimes plundered towns. This unofficial, longstanding 'war' with Spain often erupted into formal conflicts, as happened in 1739. A decade before the British had signed the Treaty of Seville, whereby they agreed not to trade with the Spain's colonies. Importantly the Spanish were also given the right in their own waters to board British vessels to verify that they were not in contravention of the Treaty. In 1731, a Spanish coast guard sloop off Havana did just that to the 'Rebecca', which was on its way from Jamaica to London. They suspected that the ship's captain, Robert Jenkins, was a privateer – someone who owned his ship and paid his crew privately but who had the tacit support of the British Government to attack foreign ships. No evidence of privateering was found but Jenkins was tortured and had one of his ears sliced off with a cutlass by a Spanish officer, who ordered the Briton to take it to King George as a token of what they had in mind for the king.

Over the next few years the tension between the two countries worsened, and in 1738 Jenkins brandished his pickled ear before the House of Commons. War fever was whipped up and a year later it was declared. One of the first actions came on 22 November 1739 when Admiral Edward Vernon led the British capture of a small silver-exporting town on the coast of what is now Panama. It was called Puerto Bello, the beautiful gate. The victory was celebrated enthusiastically, and in 1740 Vernon attended a dinner in his honour in London and at which 'God Save the King' was performed in public for the first time.

Pronounced as Portobello by the English, the London place remembers Vernon's victory, as does Portobello in Edinburgh. This recalls Portobello House built in 1755 by George Hamilton who had been present at Puerto Bello. Then there is Portobello in the West Midlands. Now part of Wolverhampton, until the reorganisation of 1966 it was part of Willenhall. It, too, must be named after the battle but unlike Edinburgh, there is no apparent link with the Central American town.

On the outstanding Wolverhampton History and Heritage Society website (www.localhistory.scit.wlv.ac.uk) Bev Page points out that there is a Vernon Close in modern Portobello, whilst Glen Miller has made clear the connection between the Black Country and the admiral. He tells me "that Hilton Park, not far away from Portobello, was the home of the Vernon family. I have always assumed that the land was part of the estate and when given over to housing was named Portobello in his honour. Portobello Tower (folly) still stands and is visible from the M6-M5 junction. Vernon was also credited for the invention of grog (a mixture of rum and water instead of raw spirit) to eke out the rum ration on long campaigns."

Portobello Tower was actually built between 1739 and 1765 to commemorate Admiral Vernon's capture of Portobello in 1739, whilst the admiral himself had been born on the Hilton Park Estate in 1684. This land had passed to the Vernon family in 1547 through marriage with the Swinnertons. In 1796 William Pitt of Pendeford wrote a general view of the 'Agriculture of the County of Stafford'. He stated that Hilton Park:

> contains plenty of flourishing oaks; and in the pleasure-grounds are some very fine ripe well-grown trees of this species, the pride of the forest: and a great variety of other timber trees grow there in the utmost luxuriance. The rides and plantations are very extensive, and furnished in the most innumerable profusion, with evidence of the planter's vigilant attention. Mr. Vernon was a very early planter, and now, in the prime of life, has the pleasure of seeing some of his first efforts in this way fast approaching towards maturity. Many of the larches, and Scotch, as well as other firs, of his planting, contain twenty feet or more timber, and are now in a very growing state.

However it was not the plantation that was to expand the fortunes of the already wealthy Vernons – rather it was deposits of coal, gravel and clay. In the twentieth century Hilton Main Colliery emphasised the significance of coal locally until it was closed down.

As for the home of the Vernons, Hilton Park Hall replaced an earlier manor house and was built in the Georgian style in about 1720 by Henry Vernon, High Sheriff of Staffordshire. The family finally sold the hall around 1951, after which it was used as a convent by the nuns of the Roman Catholic Order of St Joseph of Bordeaux and then was the head office of Tarmac Plc between 1985 and 1999. It is a Grade I listed building.

As for Portobello in the Black Country, Bev Page explains that historically it was "a small village at the western extremity of Willenhall, extending along both sides of the road from Wolverhampton to Walsall, bounded on the east and north by the River Tame. It was originally the centre of the local brick-making industry due to the plentiful supply of clay in the area. This was commemorated in the name of one of Portobello's principal streets; Brickkiln Street, which was built on an old field called Brickkiln Piece." There were also a number of mines locally and as Bev highlights Portobello "became a mining community ... The larger pits were the Osier Beds Colliery, named after the type of willow (used in basket making) that originally covered the area, Bunkers Hill Colliery, named after a battle in the American War of Independence, and Moseley Hole Colliery, named after the Moseley area which commemorates the De Mollesey (Moseley) family."

The housing in Portobello was typical of so much across the Black Country and Birmingham that was thrown up cheaply and shoddily in the Industrial Revolution and its aftermath: it was mostly back-to-back. With two bedrooms upstairs and one room downstairs, each house was part of a terrace. It was separated from its neighbours by a one-brick wall – the same depth as divided it from the house at the rear in the terrace that it backed onto. The environment was bad and public health facilities were poor. Communal washhouses and cesspits, later lavatories, were found in a party yard in which was found a pump for the supply of water.

In the mid-nineteenth century, the lack of drains, sewers and refuse collection and the want of a fresh supply of water were endemic across working-class England. This absence of sanitation was made worse by the pollution of industry. The dreadful conditions in Portobello were like those in many an urban or industrial village and were drawn powerfully and pungently by Benjamin Disraeli in his Condition of England novel, *Sybil or the Two Nations* (1845). Later a prime minister of England he was a well-informed social commentator. One section of his book focused on the centre Willenhall, or Wodgate as the author dubbed it. The situation there reflected that in Portobello and elsewhere in the west midlands:

At every fourth or fifth house, alleys seldom above a yard wide and streaming with filth, opened out of the street. These were crowded with dwellings of various size, while from the principal court often branched out a number of smaller alleys or rather narrow passages, than which nothing can be conceived more close and squalid and obscure. Here during the days of business, the sound

This photo was taken in front of 13, Brickkiln Street, Portobello, Willenhall. Thanks to Ted Pritchard. Left to right are Mrs Lister, Mrs Pitt, unknown, Mrs Parker, unknown, Jack Cotterill, (brother of Harry), Miss Kitty Gogerty, unknown, Mrs Charlotte Cotterill (mother of Harry), unknown, and Mrs Powis. It was this photo that was so important to Elizabeth Lucy Blood, nee Pitt, who now lives in Tasmania, as it shows her grandmother.

The reporter who visited Portobello in 1957 declared that "queuing for water ended years ago in most towns but not at Portobello". In one yard the tap "was shared by 35 people. Young children play in the muddy yard. In the background are the toilets and derelict houses." One lady explained that she moved into a house nearby in South Street five years before and found only a coal fire on which to cook. She then bought a gas oven but even so "the conditions here are shocking. It is impossible to keep the children clean. They have nowhere to play, only in the streets." The lady's mother, Mrs Pitt had raised a family in a small two-bedroomed house of which she had been the tenant for 35 years. She had always had to cook on a coal fire, saying that "during the summer months the small room becomes as hot as a furnace". Her rent was six shillings a week and Mrs Pitt was adamant that "I'd pay more, willingly, for a decent house".

of the hammer and the file never ceased, amid gutters of abomination and piles of foulness and stagnant pools of filth; reservoirs of leprosy and plague, whose exhalations were sufficient to taint the atmosphere of the whole kingdom and fill the country with fever and pestilence.

Just over 100 years later, in August 1957, a reporter from the *Wolverhampton Chronicle and Midland Counties Express* visited Portobello. He too was appalled by what he saw and shrank from the dreadful environment in which decent working people had to live. Many families still did not have their own water supply and had to take it from a shared pump in the yard. Houses were crumbling, walls were damp, and roofs were coming down. The atmosphere was heavy and dirty. In fact the place needed to be cleared of its bad housing. So it soon would be for Willenhall Council was set to compulsory purchase 98 houses and other properties and to demolish them.

It was a terrible indictment on England and its governments that hard-working folk were living in conditions that were no fault of their own and which had disgusted Disraeli so long ago. Yet for all the bad housing and for all the grim environment and the need to sweep them away, something was lost when Portobello was redeveloped. That sense of loss filled the soul of one local man, Harry Cotterill. Born and bred in Brickkiln Street in later life he wrote his memories of his village and began them with a stinging rebuke to redevelopment: "the powers that be decided to tear the heart out of our community in the name of the Great God of Progress. Willing or not, we were rehoused and scattered and suddenly everything was changed, was gone - buried under the steel and concrete the bulldozers left behind 1965. And it's a sure bet we lost Portobello."

It is thanks to Maureen Hunt of Slade Road, Fordhouses, Wolverhampton that I have learned about Harry. Maureen kindly wrote to me a while back after reading some recollections of Portobello in Black Country Memories. She is compiling a book "about that place called after 'The Beautiful Gateway'. Portobello is now part of Wolverhampton, not Willenhall, which comes under the Walsall Authority. I noticed from the photographs printed within this article that you have probably experienced the same difficulty as anyone else trying to locate any photographs or information about this area. Mainly that there aren't any! That is the reason that I am interested in Portobello, and so I am trying to collate all the information that is available before it disappears for all time.

"The person who really gained my interest was the late Harry Cotterill, and it is with his collection of hand written notes, with accompanying maps and family photographs, that I have got as far as I have with my compilation. Also, I have gained a deeper insight into the Brevitt and Jefcott families from Mr Ted Pritchard, who is also helping me with facts about the area of Portobello. In particular, Ted has prepared a most detailed map of all the property that the two families owned. The families

This photo brought joy to John Cotterill. It shows members of his family, including his father, Charles. Taken in 1923 the Cotterills are standing in the back yard of their house at number 13, Brickkiln Street, Portobello. Left to right are Horace, Charles, Mr Frederick Cotterill, Mrs Charlotte Cotterill with Harry in her arms, Liza, Ciss with Doris on her lap, George and Jack. In all, Harry Cotterill's parents had thirteen children but only eight lived. The lads slept in the attic, the wenches in the back room, and their mom and dad in the front room. Harry recalled that "to come downstairs every morning we had to pass through the backroom, so we had to ask if it was clear to come through – ordered by my Dad.

married up two businesses, the one family owning the pubs and shops, while the other family produced the ginger beer that was then sold in these numerous outlets.

"Harry Cotterill's notes begin with a title page, 'I was born and bred in Portobello the village I love most. Signed H. Cotterill. Born 21st June 1923. The 14th child, at number 13 Brickkiln Street, Portobello.' Amongst the hand written pages, Harry mentions 'movement of people', and goes on to say 'An introduction of this subject by the late Mrs K Rea.' Nobody living outside that community can understand how much Old Portobello meant to those who lived there. This is clearly shown in the writings of a news reporter, who went to the area to take photographs as the demolition began. Harry also paints a fuller picture of the characters mentioned in the article.

"In the newspaper article of 1957, a picture is used, looking through the remains of a window frame, in order to show a 'Beautiful Gateway!' Meaning what beautiful gateway? But to those who lived and worked there, and were brought up there, it truly was beautiful, proving that beauty really does lie in the eye of the beholder. The view through this window frame, was taken through the old shop window of Lucy Bratt's shop front. Lucy Bratt was the youngest daughter of Thomas Bratt, the Portobello Poet, who lived and worked (and wrote poetry) in this tiny shop/house. Thomas wrote in total almost 1,000 poems and sonnets, not only about local events and people but also about what was happening worldwide. I hope that the above information is of interest, Carl, as the more one looks into Old Portobello the more one can understand how the local people loved the area so much."

Harry Cotterill's reminiscences bring to the fore colourful characters who lived in his village. It seems in our sanitised and sterilised world that characters no longer have a place and are indeed shunned. In Harry's world they were at the centre of community life. Amongst them was "Aaron Brevitt, back of Brickkiln Street, lived in a small two up, two down terrace house. From his downstairs front room he used to sell sweets, milk, vegetables and other small items. Aaron only had one leg (how that came about I do not know), but he had a 'stump' fitted to enable him to walk. I can only remember seeing him out of his shop on Sunday dinner times, when he used to go with some of his mates for a drink at the 'Seven Stars' public house. Then, due to him having too much of the 'good stuff', he then had to be taken home by his mates in an old coal barrow. Aaron's mates then spent the rest of the day playing cards. Aaron kept his shop open, while he kept his a look out for 'coppers' due to the fact that gambling was taking place in his living room.

Then there was Tom Brannon of New Street. He "was the bookmaker of Portobello. He used to pay collectors (or runners) to collect the slips of papers with the bets written on them. These crude 'betting slips' would have the gambler's name, the horse's name and the amount staked. All the gamblers had a code name, in case the police caught the runner. This protected the real identity of the gambler, as at this period in time, off course betting was illegal. My brother Harry Cotterill's betting name was 'Charmo'.

"On the days of the week that racing was taking place, a runner used to take the bets from the bottom of our entry, which had a steel sewer ventilation pipe in it. The pipe was about 6ft in height with a hole in the top, and after stuffing paper to within about 6 inches from the top, he used to put his bag of betting slips within the pipe, just in case the police came around. One of the days that he had placed the bag within the pipe, someone threw a lighted match into the pipe and set the whole lot on fire, destroying all the bets. This caused an uproar when Tom Brannon found out. But he showed his honesty to the gamblers by trusting their word, and paid out in full if they said they had had a winning slip.

"Siddy Griffiths was a man of many talents. He could imitate wild birdcalls. But the thing I remember most about him was his bird catching. One day I was walking over the hills, by the side of Cottage Pool, when I saw Siddy. I went over and sat quite close to where he was, I was only seven or eight at the time, but I knew Siddy very well. He told me where to sit, as he said he was bird catching. He told me not to talk or move. Soon, overhead a flight of Linnets appeared, and Siddy started to imitate the Linnets call. Lo and behold, the Linnets started to perch in the trees all around us, close to the open traps that Siddy had prepared beforehand. As soon as he was ready, he told me to go home before he checked the traps.

"Some bird catchers used 'bird lime' to catch the birds. This was a sticky substance that used to be spread on the boughs of the trees. When the birds got stuck they used to try to escape, and while doing this, their wings got stuck, or they got hurt. And in trying to get the birds clean afterwards the chemicals that were used could damage the bird's health if not done properly. But all the times that I ever watched Siddy catch birds, he never ever used this.

"Mrs Y called 'Cockanary' was a very well known lady around the Portobello district. Whenever you went to a meeting, her name would crop up. She used to enjoy her beer drinking, fetching it from the pub in a large, half gallon, stone jar,

Portobello High Street in the 1950s, looking west towards Wolverhampton from the bridge. The first twelve houses were built to house the workers who were building the railway. In Harry Cotterill's time the sixth house along was a greengrocer's owned by Mrs Bratt – its shop window is the 'slight' bay window, just before the large dark alleyway, that led down to the railway track.

142

A tram on Summerford Road and Portobello Bridge in about 1925. Courtesy of Walsall Local History Centre, number 2034.

once or twice a night. On one of these occasions, when she was coming home from the pub, carrying the beer, she had to pass Fallon's grocery shop. There was a crowd of us lads collected there. One of the lads shouted 'Cock-Cock-anary'. Mrs Y started shouting loudly at us, with some right strong swear words. This wasn't the last we heard of it.

"I was changing myself in the living room. My mate, Joe Bristow, was waiting for me by the back door. Suddenly, a knock came at the front door and my mother went to open it. There on the doorstep, in a right temper was Mrs Y. She saw my mate Joe and called out to him in a very loud voice that he was the B… who called out about her the evening before. She started to go for him but my mother held her back. Joe opened the back door and ran as fast as his legs could carry him. (Incidentally, I can vouch that it wasn't Joe that called out as I was standing next to him).

We were about seventeen then and Joe ran straight home, and he was out of breath when he got there. His mother asked him what was up, and he told her. She put on her jacket straight away and rushed to Mrs Y's house and gave her a right telling off, and after having a good old quarrel, Mrs Y said she was sorry, and after thinking about it had got the wrong lad. But he stayed in that evening, as it had put the wind up him good and proper.

"Another incident happened when I was about nine or ten years old. It was down in the back yard of the 'Bird in Hand'. Mr Roberts had a butcher's shop in the High Street, Portobello and his slaughter house was at the back of the shop, down by the railway wall. A Mr J. Eyon was the slaughterer, and we used to watch him kill cows, pigs and sheep. When he killed the first pig he always threw the bladder out to us to blow up which we then used to play a game of football with. This was in the yard at the back of the 'Bird in Hand' pub. In this same yard were four (or five) terraced houses, one of which Mrs Y. lived in.

"While we were playing football, the Black Maria came down into the yard and stopped in front of Cockanary's door. The police got out of the van and knocked at her front door. We all gathered round to see what was going on. Mrs Y opened the door. She had not got a lot of clothing on, and she shouted in a loud voice 'If you want me, come and get me'. One of the policemen took off his cape and wrapped it around her, and pushed her back inside the house. Soon afterwards she came out with the police and was put into the Black Maria and was driven off. This caused a lot of talk within the village for the next week or two."

I thank Maureen Hunt for allowing me to see Harry's recollections and I congratulate her on her work on chronicling the people of Portobello. Maureen has two sections on the Wolverhampton History and Heritage Society website. The one is 'Snippets from Portobello's Past' and the other is 'The Portobello Poet', which focuses on the work of the Portobello Poet, Thomas Bratt. Maureen is keen to hear from anyone with memories or photos of Portobello and can be contacted via this page.